ANCIENT

Navigating the Ways of Old
to Bless the Days of New

MICHELLE GEHRT

WESTBOW
P R E S S®
A DIVISION OF THOMAS NELSON
& ZONDERVAN

WestBow Press books may be ordered through booksellers or by contacting:

WestBow Press
A Division of Thomas Nelson & Zondervan
1663 Liberty Drive
Bloomington, IN 47403
www.westbowpress.com
844-714-3454

ISBN: 978-1-6642-3228-0 (sc)
ISBN: 978-1-6642-3229-7 (hc)
ISBN: 978-1-6642-3227-3 (e)

Library of Congress Control Number: 2021908170

Print information available on the last page.

WestBow Press rev. date: 5/21/2021

"Although Michelle's text reveals the ancient paths of those gone before us, there is nothing antiquated about a faithful one who will grasp these truths and put them into practice today."

Janice Craycroft
Associate director, Victory Ministries Center of Hope

"With her book Ancient Paths, Michelle Gehrt is able to reach into the past for solid biblical truths to guide us like a compass through the unchartered waters of today. Don't feel lost and overwhelmed by today's circumstances. Instead, recalculate your walk with Christ by reclaiming God's clear directions in His Word. Add this book to your daily readings and let the fog on the horizon clear as you get back to biblical principles."

Scott McCallum
Executive director, the SHARE Mission of Columbus, Ohio
www.TheShareMission.com

"There are those that have a call to help others on their spiritual journey. Isaiah 58:12 speaks of those who will build again the old places, the foundations of past generations, and be the restorers of paths to dwell in. Michelle answered this call and literally was the vessel God used to gather together these ancient paths and foundational principles into a book. This book can set your feet upon sure paths and principles that will enable you as they did past generations to leave a mark on God's kingdom. Use this book to set your life's compass for true north so you can pursue the prize for the high calling of God in Jesus Christ."

Betty Kulich
Associate pastor, Redeemer's Church, Columbus, Ohio

Ancient Paths Navigating the Ways of Old to Bless the Days of New, will take you on a exploration through Old Testament concepts that have relevant application to our lives today. This book clearly reveals Michelle's love and passion for God's word! Her writing shed's light on truth in a way that leaves you wanting more! She brings to light the truth of God's word in a way that show's you God is the same yesterday, today and forever.

Tammy Bennett, Pastor
Redeemer's Church
Columbus Ohio

To the one who desires to follow the ancient paths of those who have gone before us and who hunger to live aligned with the Father while fulfilling the calling of your destinies. My prayer for you is that you will see the Father's heart and His love for you, and that by being in tune with the Lord, you will walk out your faith in life boldly with the power and authority that God originally designed for your life. Come, Holy Spirit, guide each finger along these Spirit-filled pages and impart to each reader the wisdom and discernment to know you in a more intimate way. Establish their ways upon these ancient paths.

Contents

Foreword

Writing a foreword for a book is a great honor, and I am pleased to have the opportunity to write one for Michelle Gehrt's second book, *Ancient Paths*. I first met Michelle about four years ago when I was giving a series of talks on a book I had written. Since that time, Michelle has published two books of her own. The first was a devotional entitled *Behold! God Is Speaking to Us*, which she published in 2019.

Michelle's second book, *Ancient Paths*, is an inspirational book in which she exhorts her readers to follow the tried and true ancient paths that were followed by the biblical heroes depicted in the Old and New Testaments. In this book, she also exhorts us to turn aside from the superficiality that characterizes so much of modern Christianity. Michelle points out that many Christians have become stuck after accepting Jesus Christ as their Savior and receiving water baptism. However, she convincingly demonstrates that there is so much more to be experienced in the Christian life, and she encourages her readers to follow in the footsteps of the men and women of God who have followed the ancient paths.

Michelle emphasizes that "finding your true self, whom God made you to be, is more important than anything else." Actually, we find that our heavenly Father has a unique plan and purpose for each of us. Moreover, He has written His plan in a book for each of us, declaring the works that He has ordained for us to fulfill, as the apostle Paul declared: "For we are His workmanship, created in Christ Jesus for good works, which God prepared beforehand so that we would walk in them" (Ephesians 2:10).

However, Michelle also stresses that God's plan for our lives can only be realized as we continue to follow the ancient paths traversed by the saints who went before us. She emphasizes that God is the same yesterday, today, and forever. Therefore, the ancient paths pursued by the saints of the Old and New Testaments have not been changed or superseded by modern developments.

In this book, the reader will find that the first step in following the ancient paths is repentance. However, true repentance is not a one-time occurrence but a path to be pursued throughout our entire lives. Michelle also places an emphasis on learning to live our lives in this world while embracing the heavenly paths followed by the saints who went before us. Other topics covered in this book include prayer, fasting, enlightenment, prophecy, dreams, visions, and journaling.

I personally found her book to be both inspiring and challenging. Therefore, I am pleased to recommend this book to everyone reading this. However, *Ancient Paths* will be especially helpful to the person seeking to follow our Lord in the ways of the deeper Christian life.

—Gary K. Larson, Bible teacher and author of *The Apostolic Mission of Jesus the Messiah* and *The Spirit Who Makes You Sons*

Acknowledgments

First and foremost, I would like to thank the Lord for inspiring me to write this book, for giving me the courage to keep taking steps, and for keeping me in alignment with Him to write what was on His heart for the world. I would like to thank my husband for standing by my side for yet another book and for showing me things from his perspective to encourage new insight while writing. Thank you, Gary Larson, my friend and fellow author of *The Apostolic Mission of Jesus the Messiah*, for the time you have put in to be my second set of eyes and for your biblical knowledge that has been a tremendous help. A special thanks goes out to my friend Betty, author of *The River*, for all your insight and inspiration along the way. We have been on this journey together as we have been obedient to the call of writing for the Lord. Lastly, I would like to thank the reader for walking these ancient paths that have been lost throughout history and leaving your footprint for the generations to come, living in God's intended ways for this life.

Introduction

For some time I had been having a stirring from within, a nudge from the Holy Spirit to write this book. As I read through the Old Testament and studied the ancient ones who have gone before us, my heart began to feel a heaviness. I was filled with astonishment and admiration to see these ones of long ago and how they were discovering faith at levels that we don't often see today. Through this reflection, I heard the Holy Spirit whisper in my ear to walk these ancient paths. It was through being quarantined in 2020 due to the coronavirus that the Holy Spirit touched me, and I began finding scripture after scripture and chasing after those who went before us that *Ancient Paths* was birthed. God inspired me to write this book to show others who He is and to draw people back into relationship with Him. We have veered off the ancient paths and become lost in our ways. Our Father has left us the ancient manual, the scriptures, to guide us back to Him. As we humbly surrender ourselves to Him and His Word we find eternal fulfillment. The greatest gift that God gave us was His Son dying on the cross. It is through Jesus that we are redeemed and made new. Our righteousness comes when we accept Jesus and choose to live the way that God intended for us. When we honor the Lord through prayer, supplication, and petition, hearing from God and walking out the call, we see that "Thy will be done on earth as it is in heaven" (Matthew 6:10 NKJV). This is the basis for everything, and we get to partake in seeing it all come into fruition! Our Father loves us so much that He wants us to walk side by side with Him and the ancients of long ago. These are the ways that we must get back to. Together, you and I will walk these ancient paths and glean the mysteries of those who have gone before us.

The ancient paths are the unique routes of those who followed God. They chose to walk out the calling God had for them over their lives. They chose the good way. When you follow the ancient paths, you are chasing after the narrow way.

> *Your Eyes saw my substance, being yet unformed.*
> *And in Your book they all were written,*
> *The days fashioned for me, when as yet there were none of them.*
> *(Psalm 139:16 NKJV)*

Your identity began before God created you. It began when you were just a book, and God was preparing a way for you. He knew you before you were in the womb, and He has great plans for your destiny. Finding your true self, whom God made you to be, is more important than anything else. When you find your God-given identity, you will start to see how everything else comes into place. God has revealed throughout scripture what He has for us and what He wants to give us to walk as true sons and daughters helping to manifest God's plans on earth. You are vessels carrying the glory of God.

Jesus was on a mission when He came to earth. He too had a book written in heaven. Hebrews 10:5–7 (NKJV) states,

> *Therefore, when He came into the world, He said:*
> *"Sacrifice and offering You did not desire,*
> *But a body You have prepared for Me.*
> *⁶ In burnt offerings and sacrifices for sin*
> *You had no pleasure.*
> *⁷ Then I said, 'Behold, I have come—*
> *In the volume of the book it is written of Me—*
> *To do Your will, O God.'"*

We too are on a mission to continue the workings of Jesus, who is now carrying on His work in the heavenly ministry, while doing greater things. Walking out our destiny causes change to occur in the atmosphere. This is where we see a shift and are walking out our assignments in alignment with what God planned for us, heaven invading earth through us.

The Holy Spirit is active and available to you. God says He will pour out His Spirit on all people. What was revealed to Joel over two thousand years ago, and what Peter quoted in the book of Acts, has now come forth to us through Jesus Christ today. Do you have the courage to rise up and move forward as royalty; part of God's family, to show the world the promise of what God has planned? Are you thirsty for more of what God has for you? Do you need a kick-start or fresh eyes to see all the revelation of what God has in store for your destiny? Can you feel it in your bones, but somehow you feel stuck? Dry bones shall rise again! Ezekiel 37:1–14 is about the prophet Ezekiel getting a vision from God of dry bones and the assignment that God tells Ezekiel to carry out. He was to restore and bring the Israelites into the land of Israel. God wants to replenish you today!

Ancient Paths has been designed to show you what a life looks like when you are living your full potential with the Holy Spirit— that is, the power of the Holy Spirit and the effects it has upon your life. This book is for people who feel they have been stuck at baptism and have not been able to move forward, but they want to move forward in giving their lives to the Lord. In these Spirit-filled pages, you will learn to hear the voice of God, walk in the Spirit, and experience and move in signs and miracles. You will learn alignment with God, and your faith will grow. Journaling will be your helper along the way. You will also learn the importance of writing down prophetic words that people have spoken over you and your life. Your prayer life will deepen by learning to pray effectively from power and authority and also moving to stand in the gap for others through intercessory prayer. You will see how fasting opens doors of new opportunity and shows you the next steps of moving forward in the kingdom of God. Each chapter is a preparation to show you how to live and move in a Spirit-filled life with the power of the Holy Spirit within you. You will also learn to "fight the good fight of faith" (1 Timothy 6:12 NKJV) and wage spiritual warfare while liberating the captives of the devil.

Join me on this journey as we begin to open our eyes, see scales falling off, and move from the natural into the supernatural realm. Our true struggle and warfare lies here in the unseen. We will go deep beneath the surface and start to move supernaturally in this world but not of it, living in two realms at once to fulfill God's plan and our purpose here on earth. Grab your Bible, the instruction manual for your life, and press in and onward to learn more about your destiny in the kingdom. You were made for more!

Chapter 1

Ancient Paths

Thus says the Lord:
"Stand in the ways and see,
And ask for the old paths, where the good way is,
And walk in it;
Then you will find rest for your souls.
But they said, 'We will not walk in it.'
—Jeremiah 6:16 (NKJV)

The term *ancient paths* refers to those who followed God and walked out His calling on their lives. The Ancient of Days is the One who directs the ancient pathways that we too walk on. This is seen in the book of Daniel.

I watched till thrones were put in place,
And the Ancient of Days was seated;
His garment was white as snow,
And the hair of His head was pure like wool.
His throne was a fiery flame,
Its wheels a burning fire. (Daniel 7:9 NKJV)

Our God is the Ancient of Days. He is the same today as He was yesterday and will be in the days to come. Our Father holds the key to our lives. Through alignment with Him, He directs our paths. By following the ancient paths, we too will leave our marks for the next generation. By fulfilling our books written in heaven, one day we will take our place on these paths, being established as ancient ones.

There are many paths to take in life, but when we follow the ancient paths, we are following the good way of those who went before us. Jesus laid the foundation and set a pattern for us to follow. Then many followed in the footsteps of Jesus, and some continue to do so to this day. You are part of God's plan, and these ancient paths are also for you! These ancients passed on tools to us for encouragement to help us to keep pushing ahead while never losing sight of the final destination.

As we tread upon these old paths, through studying God's Word, we begin to fulfill the calling of our lives by foreseeing His will and purpose, just as the ones before us saw. Our vision becomes unveiled, making our eyes clear to see these particular patterns forming in front of us as we step along the way. This is how we begin to learn, grow, and mature. God begins to transform us into His original design. As we veer from our own way and onto the pathway of the Ancient of Days, we become well established in carrying the testimony of our King!

The uniqueness of this pattern reveals to us a life of faithfulness and increases the more we step into our divine calling. The aged-ones left evidence in the Bible concerning the patterns for us to follow. There are right and wrong paths we can take. Through reading the Word of God and prayer, along with the Holy Spirit, who gives us knowledge and discernment, we can align ourselves to become whole with the Father. Our alignment will enable us to live righteously and move in the power and authority that God wants to give us. Alignment comes when we seek the will of God, not the power of God. When we seek the will of God, His power and authority that

He has designed for us will manifest through us for the glory of God and His kingdom. Our thirst for more of Him will shift the atmosphere, and the Holy Spirit will flow from us.

The Bible is the living Word of God and a road map to position us into completeness. Jesus, our High Priest; Joel; Peter; and the prophets who have gone before us set unique patterns and paths for us. Through Jesus, we receive our salvation and the presence of the Holy Spirit. He comes to live in us and fill us with the power to do greater things. It's up to us to thirst or hunger for more than our ordinary, everyday lives. God has so much more for us. Through growing closer to the Lord in relationship, prayer, and study, more is given to us. The Bible is like a matrix or a puzzle. Everything we need is found in His Word and unlocks wisdom that we need to follow. Luke 24:45 (TPT) states, "He supernaturally unlocked their understanding to receive the revelation of the Scriptures."

Jesus made the scriptures visible to their minds so that they would understand what He was telling them about what was to come. Just as we have our natural senses, we also have our spiritual senses waiting to be opened to see the goodness of what God has in store for us. Are you hungry? Are you ready to ask God to unveil your spiritual eyes of understanding?

Prophecy is throughout the Bible, and when we have a yearning or desire, we get glimpses of what God is revealing. Our new eyes open the closer we become to God. As we get into alignment with the Father, the Holy Spirit begins to move. It is the power of the Holy Spirit within us that moves to carry out the will of God. This is when we begin to step into our destinies, being guided by the Spirit and fulfilling the work and ministry of His Son, Jesus Christ.

God is seeking fellowship with us, and He shows us this throughout the Bible. The Bible is all about God's covenant with us. These covenants of promises confirm His intended restoration among people and how we will be redeemed. *The Apostolic Mission of Jesus the Messiah* by Gary Larson is a good book that goes into great depth on this information. He is the Great Redeemer. He restores, delivers, and heals us. It is we who break the covenant with our Father over and over again. Through Jesus Christ taking on our sins, we are made new in Him. God is gracious and full of mercy. He loves us even in our sin. He promises us to never leave or forsake us (Deuteronomy 31:6). Our Father created us to need Him as a helper. He has given us everything we need to sustain life on earth and to fulfill the assignments that are written in our books.

God remains faithful. He has given us His manual and wants us to follow the ancient paths. When you follow these paths, you are following the narrow way. The narrow way is a place that many pass by, but this path has the unction to function. This way is where we can live in the anointing of the manifesting presence of God. Following those of long ago will take you to another level. Isaiah states,

> *Those from among you*
> *Shall build the old waste places;*
> *You shall rise up the foundations of many generations;*
> *And you shall be called the Repairer of the Breach,*
> *The Restorer of Streets to Dwell In. (Isaiah 58:12 NKJV)*

By following the way of old, we will learn the good way and walk out God's plan. Isaiah 58:12 tells us that as Christians, we will repair what has been broken. We will set forth to reach the lost and fulfill the Great Commission (see Matthew 28:16–20 NKJV.) This is the calling on our lives. The scripture tells us what we will do, and to do this, we need a map or a pathway. Ancient paths hold the key to reaching your destiny. Ancient paths have been lost to the church over time due to our own human logic or understanding. The latest and the greatest have taken priority. We need to get back to the basics by remembering who we are in the Father and what He has in store for us as carriers of His Word.

Ancient Paths

Those who went before us have set their feet on these same paths. We have the opportunity today to follow their journey. As we follow in their footsteps, we will learn to discern as the ancients did and follow the path of God. This will enable us to see these unique patterns and walk in the ways of the old. The Bible is a timeline of what has happened and what is to come. We are living in biblical times today, and we have been given the tools in the Bible to walk out and continue these age-old ways. There is a sequence in the scriptures, and when we truly hunger and surrender ourselves to the Father, we will be positioned for more. The ancients who have gone before us were chasing after God just as we pursue Him today. When we take the wisdom passed on from our elders, we too can make our way back to Him and fulfill our destinies. God wants to show us and give us much more than what we can see with our earthly eyes. He wants us to walk into our destinies. God has prepared the way for us. Are you prepared to walk in the ancient ways of those who went before you?

Father, we come to You today to receive all that You have for us. We are thankful that You have left us these ancient paths to tread upon. Just as our forefathers have taken steps to grow closer to You by continuing to move forward in all Your ways, searching You out, we too hunger to walk aligned with You. Father, we ask You to show us something new through these Spirit-filled pages that will confirm within us Your revelations. We know that the world is rapidly changing day by day and getting further from Your ancient ways, and we know that You want to see a return. Use us, Father, to help gather the harvest. We want to fulfill our callings You have for us to glorify You and Your kingdom. We ask You to activate and cause a stirring inside us. As sons and daughters, we thank You for Your Spirit that guides and leads us along the way. We love You and thank You for the tools You have left behind. Put forth an urge within us to dig deep into Your Word to help us reflect the image of

Your Son while we walk along these ancient paths. Help us to remain close to You. Show us through prayer and supplication how to live righteous, aligned with You while spreading the good news. Help us to also love the way You do and make us a light on the path for all to see. Use us as we are vessels for only You. Come, Holy Spirit.

Notes

1. Gary Larson, *The Apostolic Mission of Jesus the Messiah,* Tampa: Xulon, 2016

Chapter 2

Ancient of Days: His Design for Us

The Ancient Ways of the Spirit of God

In the beginning God created the heavens and the earth. The earth
was without form, and void; and darkness was on the face of the
deep. And the Spirit of God was hovering over the face of the waters.
—*Genesis 1:1–2 (NKJV)*

The Ancient of Days had a plan for creation and knew precisely how
it all would come about. His plan was brought forth with the help of
the Holy Spirit to awaken the world, bringing life and vitality to it.
With the aid of the Holy Spirit, creation came into existence. When
we take a closer look at Genesis 1:2, we see that the Spirit of God
was hovering over the face of the waters. Let's investigate the word
hover. In this scripture, the Hebrew word *rachaph* is translated in
English as *hover*. The only other time this word appears to be used
in this context is in Deuteronomy 32:11 (NKJV). When we look at
the context of how *rachaph* was used in these books, *hover* is meant
to describe what birds do to protect their babies in their nests. The
Spirit of God was hovering over the waters, protecting creation. God

used His Spirit to breathe life into creation and humanity. This is the first way that we see the Holy Spirit at work, co-laboring with God.

Throughout the Old Testament, we see the movement and life of the Holy Spirit. The Holy Spirit came upon individuals, and even a donkey, at different times for different purposes. God used the Holy Spirit for prophecy, knowledge, guidance, warnings, and equipping, to show who He is and more. Supernatural powers were given to the ancient ones to carry out assignments of the Lord. We see this when we read about warriors in battle, judges, priests, prophets, and kings. The Spirit of God came upon them to help them accomplish what they couldn't on their own. God also used the Holy Spirit to show the people who He was. The Spirit empowered, taught, led, set battle plans, made evil known, established believers, and gave special skills and talents to these ancients. The holiness of God was also shown through those who were used as mouthpieces for the Lord, dwelling on them for a period of time to carry out His plans. Just about anywhere you look in the Old Testament, you will see the power of the Holy Spirit at work. We will examine some of those who went before us to see how God was at work, using His Spirit to put things into motion. The great designer was making a way then and now for us through this same Spirit.

Let's take a look at Aaron, the first Hebrew high priest of the Old Testament, and how God gave him supernatural knowledge and discernment to carry out his position. God instructed Moses to appoint Aaron to the high priest position so that He could minster to him. Along with this divine calling, God gave Moses a set of detailed instructions to enable Aaron to fulfill his mission in God. All the qualifications of Aaron were established during this time, and his feet began to tread the ancient paths, making way for the ones who would follow him. Aaron was obedient to the calling. Aaron was chosen by God to represent Him and was the intermediary between the people of Israel and God. Aaron wore a breastplate, among others things, as part of his attire. On this breastplate were twelve stones representing the twelve tribes of Israel. This breastplate would help Aaron answer the people's queries and help him in prayer with the Lord. Inside the breastplate, the Urim and Thummin were placed. This is where we begin to see the Spirit of God at work. The Urim and Thummin were the means by which God gave guidance to Aaron for Israel. Somehow these stones would answer crucial questions posed by the high priest concerning the tribes of Israel, revealing yes or no answers. Aaron was able to perceive certain things through the Urim and Thummin that only God would know. This is how the power of the Holy Spirit was moving in and through Aaron. David was also known to use the Urim and Thummin; we see this in 1 Samuel 23:1–9, focusing on verse 9. Many times these answers would come as a yes or a no, and at other times the Lord spoke directly. In these days, this was the way the Spirit of God functioned. Only God can perform a supernatural work such as this. God is full of surprises and has great things in store for us to receive, if only we will believe. God wants us to live supernaturally with Him and receive all the gifting's He has in store for us. When we read the Bible, we gain knowledge of the ancients who went before us. God wants us to walk on these ancient paths and see the goodness of who He is. He is the same that He was yesterday, today, and tomorrow.

In Exodus 31:1–5, God filled people with the His Spirit to give knowledge, talent, and craftsmanship to build the Tabernacle that would carry the presence of the Lord. In Numbers 27:18, the Lord instructed Moses to lay hands on Joshua through impartation to give him the qualifications that he needed to be governor. God used Nehemiah to rebuild the walls in Jerusalem. Nehemiah wept, fasted, and interceded for the people. God heard his burdens and answered his prayers to restore the people of Israel. We see the works of the Holy Spirit throughout these ancient days of the Old Testament repeatedly. There are many fascinating stories of those of old who were carriers of the Spirit of God. If you hunger to know more about those who went before you, take a Selah moment. Pause and reflect on the books of Numbers, Judges, Job, Daniel, Joel, Micah, and Haggai, just to name a few; Spirit of God encounters.

God, the Great Architect, has a design for all things—including you!

Before Pentecost

> *And it shall come to pass afterward That I will pour*
> *out My Spirit on all flesh; Your sons and your daughters*
> *shall prophesy, Your old men shall dream dreams, Your*
> *young men shall see visions. (Joel 2:28 NKJV)*

God activated the Holy Spirit in the Old Testament to engage people and to prophesy what was to come. The Holy Spirit did not always remain upon these people from long ago. In Numbers 11:25, the Spirit of God rested on the seventy elders to prophesy and afterward never came upon them to prophesy again. One place in particular that we see this is in the book of Joel. The prophet Joel believed in the promises of God, and therefore the Holy Spirit dwelt in him to move for the Lord. He exhorted the nation of Israel to turn back to their first love. We may not know much about Joel in terms of times and dates, but we do know that he was used by God to bring the nation of Israel to repentance. This is a key theme that we see throughout the Bible, leading up to today. God was calling His people to repent then, just like He is calling us to do today, in order to make atonement for our sins. What was once true of the ancients stands as a credible source for us today.

Joel heard the voice of the Lord and acted upon it. God spoke through many ancients of long ago this same way. Today, God speaks to us through His Son (see Hebrews 1:1–3 NKJV). When we read the Bible, we receive life through it. In 2 Timothy 3:16 (NKJV), Paul states, "All Scripture is God-breathed and is useful for teaching, rebuking, correcting and training in righteousness." The Bible is a gift from the Lord for us today, to learn to walk in His ways as heirs. The Spirit of God carried Joel, and he spoke prophecies according to the will of God. As we unyieldingly dedicate ourselves to reading the Bible, more will open up to us and through the process of maturation, and we will come into our destinies that have been predestined by the Lord. When we pass along these events that the ancient ones have passed to us through scriptures, not only does it stir our faith to believe, but also an impartation takes place to receive all that the Father has for us. These authentic, Spirit-filled pages are tools to equip us today and for future generations to come.

When we read scripture, we are walking in the paths and ways of those who went before us. Our faith increases the activation of our spiritual ability to move supernaturally through our gifting's to prophesy, dream, and more. Our Father has an inheritance that He wants to give us. This inheritance is not just for the ancient ones but is available to us today. His promises stand true and remain forever. Bible days are not as ancient as you think, because we are still living in them today. We have failed to follow after the ancient ways and instead have chosen to blindly follow our own way. This route has led us, and continues to lead us, into the same course as those who were not in harmony with the Father. Of course, our circumstances will look different, but the underlying cause is the same. It all revolves around what God has been trying to show us from the beginning. The Lord created us to be in union with Him. We are the covenant breakers, and not much has changed since the beginning of time. Even though destruction continues to come, God still loves us and never leaves us. The problems lie within our own eyes. The ways of the world have a way of enticing us just as the enemy sees fit for us individually.

Father, we thank You for Your goodness and Your firm hand on us. We come to You today seeking Your forgiveness and asking You to show us what it is that we may be missing. We ask for forgiveness of our sins and to deliver us from the continuation of the sins of the world. Father, we ask You to bring us out of this present darkness into Your care. Father, we are found in You because you are merciful, wondrous, loving, kind, tender, and strong. You are our protector and our refuge in all times. You, O Lord, are our umbrella who shields us from all rain. We love You and ask You to come, come now, Holy Spirit. Lead us into what is true and right. Give our eyes understanding beyond our conscience recollection and show us how to move freely with Your Spirit in and on us. We surrender to You fully. Come, Holy Spirit.

Joel foretold what would happen in the future through the prophecy the Lord gave him. This prophecy came to pass many years later, as seen in the book of Acts 2:1–4, 16–21 (NKJV), the coming of the Holy Spirit at Pentecost. Joel told us in Joel 2:28 (NKJV) that this outpouring of the Holy Spirit would not be just for the church but for everyone. However, before this prophecy could be fulfilled, things needed to be put into order. One thing in particular needed to happen; namely, everyone needed to repent. This was the calling of John the Baptist, the forerunner of Jesus Christ the Messiah. He was preparing the way for Jesus by telling people that they needed to repent and be baptized for the final judgment that was to come. God has a design for all of us. We are all uniquely crafted in His image. It is up to us to follow the unique patterns that sets us apart from the world and gets us on the narrow path. This path is the way to the Father. It is the way to wholeness. Our completion is within the Lord.

This whole theme of repenting is significant for us today, for our future and our future generations to come. You see, we were created to be in union with God. We need to get back to the elemental foundations of how He intended the world to be. We need to get back to our first love by setting our hearts right. He will protect us and keep us safe, and His eyes will never leave us. The world cannot fulfill us in the same way as the Father. When we veered off, we not only lost our way but also lost everything that was given to us. When we closed our eyes to those who went before us, the ancient paths and patterns began to get covered up by roots, and our eyes could no longer see the narrow dirt path. The good way was hidden in our sin and the sin of the world. We have lost synchronicity with the Father. The good news is that it is never too late. We have such a merciful and gracious Father. He is in the stillness, in the waiting. Today, we have the opportunity through Jesus Christ our Savior to come to our Father and stand boldly in His presence as sons and daughters of God! When we repent as in the ways of old, we are ridding ourselves of what prevents our eyes from seeing what is to become of us. We are the light of the world. We all have books written in heaven, and when we come into union, in alignment with the Father, our books begin operating in the designed ways of the Great Architect. The supernatural ways of the kingdom are now engaged, on full throttle, and we can begin to labor joyfully in the fruits of the Lord!

By following the ancient paths of those who went before us, we will be leading our lives the way that God arranged for us. We can see this through many of the ancients who have gone before us. Through this new advantage, we will obtain new knowledge from the Father, living from a place of union in and with Him. Finally we can see the world as God designed it to be from His kingdom view. Kingdom-minded people living in the dominion of earth from a heavenly perspective! Take in the sweet-smelling aroma of the Lord by letting your fingers do the walking, flipping the pages of the ancients while your eyes wonder through the sacred writings of the Bible.

Pentecost

When the Day of Pentecost had fully come, they were all with one accord in one place. And suddenly there came a sound from heaven, as of a rushing mighty wind, and it filled the whole house where they were sitting. Then there appeared to them divided tongues, as of fire, and one sat upon each of them. And they were all filled with the Holy Spirit and began to speak with other tongues, as the Spirit gave them utterance. (Acts 2:1-4 NKJV)

But this is what was spoken by the prophet Joel:

"And it shall come to pass in the last days, says God,
That I will pour out of My Spirit on all flesh; Your
sons and your daughters shall prophesy,
Your young men shall see visions, Your old men shall dream dreams.
And on My menservants and on My maidservants I will
pour out My Spirit in those days; And they shall prophesy.
I will show wonders in heaven above And signs in the
earth beneath: Blood and fire and vapor of smoke.
The sun shall be turned into darkness, And the moon into blood,
Before the coming of the great and awesome day of the Lord. And
it shall come to pass That whoever calls on the name of the Lord
Shall be saved." (Acts 2:16–21 NKJV)

The Day of Pentecost was the day when the Holy Spirit descended upon the disciples and other followers of Jesus. What a miraculous day! The Holy Spirit came to permanently live in those who believed and were called to greater works for the kingdom of God. Upon the arrival of the Holy Spirit, Jesus gave the disciples instructions to follow. In Acts 1:4, He told them not to leave Jerusalem until the Father sends them the gift, which He had promised. That gift was the Holy Spirit. They needed the Spirit of God to do things outside of their own abilities. Jesus's work was not finished, and there was much more to do. With the help of the Comforter, we become witnesses of Jesus Christ conformed to His image. This Helper is not something that will depart from us, but He remains in us forever because the Savior of the world paid the ultimate price. Throughout the process of sanctification, over the course of our lives, we will bear the good fruit claiming our intended victory over the sins of the world as Jesus continues doing greater things in the heavenlies. The Holy Spirit gives us power and authority to move supernaturally, changing lives and gathering the harvest on earth. We essentially are living in two realms at once because the Spirit of God in us gives us direct access to our Father in the spirit realm.

God wants to make a change in the world. This change comes from having a hunger for the Lord. We need to move from hearing about what the Lord says at Sunday service to having a direct encounter with the Lord as witnesses and begin to take bold steps of faith out of obedience. When we move, action takes place, and we are never the same. Peter's life was changed forever with his encounter with the Holy Spirit. He preached the first church sermon. The subject of his message was the theme we see throughout the entire Bible leading up to today: repent. To receive, we must repent and ask Him to come into our hearts to make us pure and new. The Holy Spirit is available to all who believe today. Part of God's design was to make the Holy Spirit available to us so we can move in one accord with the Father. If we are part of the family of the kingdom of God, then God wants to give us all that He has for us. Just like a parent on earth who wants the best for their children, our heavenly Father wants even greater things for you! Receiving the goodness of the Lord starts with a choice and then belief.

The Bible says that divided tongues of fire sat upon each one of the disciples. This visualization of what occurred at that moment was seen and heard in the believers. The fire was how the Holy Spirit consumed and purified the people. I am sure that you have come across people today who are on fire with God. They carry a different kind of presence. They shine from the inside out, and simply being near them makes you want to have what they have. They radiate the Father's love because it cannot be contained. Their love is contagious. This is what it is to be filled with the Holy Spirit. Before you encounter them, you are living your usual, mundane life, but when you come in contact with these Spirit-filled believers of God, you sense a feeling of love like you're the only person around. It is a feeling of pure devotion. You can feel the Father's love beaming out from the believers. Although this experience barely touches what the disciples experienced that day, this is just one example that can help you relate. The Holy Spirit is falling on people today as we speak, and many supernatural encounters are occurring. People are being slain in the Spirit. They are experiencing the love of God in many different ways. Not only does the Father want for you to receive this gift, but He also has so many more gifts for you. When you receive the Father's love, you will never be the same. He wants to give you everything that He has to reach the world. He will give you some things meant only for you to fill you up, and He will share with you other things meant for the entire world. His filling is everlasting. You will be like a sponge that keeps soaking in His goodness until you overflow. When you get into that place of overflow, you begin to pour out His glory. This is the grace that God has given you to extend to others. The oil from heaven has been poured into your being as you receive His divine power. With this power, you can release it unto the world, sharing with all and having this same experience through committing to live a life through Jesus Christ. If we recall, John baptized with water, but God baptizes with His Spirit. John prepared the way for something greater to come. Today is the day the Lord has made, and He gives us this day to come to Him and receive His greatness and glory for the world. We are His generals, watchmen, heirs, sons, and daughters sent with a purpose a calling from heaven. We have been chosen and hold a place at the table of the Lord. We have been fashioned in His liking according to His plans for His purpose. With the help of the Holy Spirit, we can fulfill what has been written for us, obtaining the place of special honor with the Father.

Can you imagine living during the time of Pentecost? What started out as the Holy Spirit touching the lives of 120 people quickly increased to thousands. Peter preached his first sermon, and three thousand more people were converted. The gift of tongues manifested, and people from all parts of the world heard the disciples speaking their own language! God provided this miracle to the believers to see His greatness, and this miracle allowed for them to hear and understand what was being said. All the gifts that were given to the ancient ones are available to us today, except of course the office gifts seen in Ephesians 4, which are given by God. God calls them specifically. You will know if you are one of the people called to the offices.

As we read through scripture and see the mighty works of God, we begin to obtain a newfound hope and faith. This radical faith can be shared with others through our generosity. This is how we partner with the Lord to see His kingdom come. Stories of the ancients were passed down from generation to generation before there was technology to speed things up. We have lost this sense due to the ever-increasing, rapid growth of the world, ways of the world, and views of what we should be spreading or how we should be living our lives. We have forgotten the simple ways of the world. Our lens has become smudged with the newest thing. We have lost all clarity, and our sense of being has become what the world says we are. We are missing the focal point of our lives. God never changes—we do. We change with the wind. Recollecting the stories of those of old is what keeps us connected to the Vinedresser. We need to get back to the ancient ways and start treading our feet upon these old paths, following after those who followed after the heart of God.

Do not remove the ancient landmark
Which your fathers have set. (Proverbs 22:28 NKJV)

Ancient boundaries are spiritual kingdom matters set up by God. These fences or guardrails that were put into place by the Word of God should have never been moved. Everything that the Father does is for His children. He is our great Protector. We have lost the ways of old and need to remember who we are and where our place is. The ancient ways of long ago are still meant for today. Even though the world is constantly changing, we are to be grounded in God's unchanging Word. Cultural pressures should not make us cave but only to dig deeper into the Word of God and stand firm on His promises. When we change the ancient boundaries to reflect the world we live in today, conforming to those pressures only hurt us, and pain and destruction can come forth. Proverbs 22:28 mirrors what is said in Deuteronomy 19:14. God shows us the original design that He meant for all of humanity in the Bible. We are part of this design. We have lost our ways, falling into the ways of the world. Our authority does not lie in moving the ancient boundaries of those who went before us. Our authority lies and rests on the Word of God, which we are to share with the world. We need to rewind and set our feet on the ancient paths, going back to the expertise of those who went before us. By creating our own path to tread upon, we risk our way. We were never meant to take upon the world as if it was our own; instead, we were made to co-labor with God, who designed the patterns and ways for us to live. The good news is that our salvation through Jesus Christ and the gift of the infilling of His Spirit sets us back into the original boundaries set for us from the beginning of time. Receive today what God has for you written in your books in heaven. Rejoice in the power of the Holy Spirit to lead and guide you. Allow the Lord to set you on fire. As you begin this transformation, turning back the hand of time and following the good, simple way, know that you are loved and set aside for the purpose of God!

Father, we love You so much and hunger for more of You. Help us to move from what looks like the law to moving to the tune of who You are. Help us to have an outflow of Your Spirit to change lives right before our eyes! For we know that You have commissioned us to go and move by spreading the good news. Without You or the Holy Spirit within us, we would not have the strength and endurance to run the race to the end. We know that with You, we can do all things and nothing is impossible. We thank You for Your Son, who died for us to live. We thank You that when He departed, the Holy Spirit came. We ask that You fill us today with Your Spirit. Release Your presence to us; we long to see You. Make us more like You. We thank You so much for leaving Your Spirit to have many encounters throughout our journeys as we tread the ancient paths of those who have gone before us. We believe! Our faith is ever increasing to what You are doing in and through us. We fully surrender to You. May You have Your way with us, and may we, as vessels, fulfill our destinies that You have written for us in our books in heaven. Father, we ask You to pour Your Spirit out over us. May You direct all our ways. May we be established with You. We love and honor You, our King. May You, our Father, receive all the glory! Come, Holy Spirit.

Salvation through Jesus

In the past God spoke to our ancestors through the prophets at many times and in various ways, but in these last days he has spoken to us by his Son, whom he appointed heir of all things, and through whom also he made the universe. (Hebrews 1:1–2 NIV)

Joel prophesied a disclosure of what came true centuries later in Acts, the church age. This same prophecy came true for us through Jesus Christ. It is time to turn away from the ways of the world by setting our eyes on Jesus. There is only one way to the Father, and that is through His Son. Through repenting and accepting Him, we receive the gift of salvation. Jesus, our High Priest, was part of God's design for the world. He paid the ultimate price for us to live. He became sin and took it on in exchange for us to carry on His works. Now, Jesus stands at the right hand of the Father doing greater things in the heavenlies (Acts 7:55–56).

Watch over each other to make sure that no one misses the revelation of God's grace. And make sure no one lives with a root of bitterness sprouting within them which will only cause trouble and poison the hearts of many. (Hebrews 12:15 TPT)

A hardened heart not only causes suffering for the individual but also has the potential to spread onto others. Repenting is so important. We need to be able to identify these weak linings that the enemy tries to infiltrate. Asking for forgiveness not only makes us pure and cleanses our hearts but also blocks the enemy from access to our thoughts and more. When times such as these come, be on guard and look to Jesus. God's will is being done in all times in our lives, and through faith we believe this. With our eyes on Jesus at all times, we will not conform to the ways of the world; instead, we will be transformed into the likeness of the Father. Roots are strong and often hard to pull from the ground. They strangle other plants and kill off everything in the flowerbed. When the root gets out of control, it spreads among those closest to it, leaving them lifeless. God sent Jesus to take away the roots in our lives. The gift of being able to go to the Lord through prayer and petitioning our strongholds of the enemy shows us how much God loves us. God wants to deal with any old roots in your life. He wants to replace these roots with His everlasting love. God is full of grace and mercy and prevails over evil. His hand never leaves us. His love is constant, never changing. We have to make the first step, repent, and prepare for things to come. Throughout scripture we find that judgment will come, and that is why it is important to go to the Father for forgiveness. One day Jesus will come back for His Church, for all the believers. Salvation through Jesus makes it possible for us to have a complete transformation and have eternal life with the Father through His Son.

The great act that Jesus came to do made it easier for us to reach the Father. Instead of being under the law, God wrote the new covenant on our hearts. Jesus brings us into the presence of God. He made it much easier for us to follow the way of the Lord. We are saved when we choose to come to Jesus. We can bring all our baggage. God is not looking at our sin or us, but He is looking at the offering that we bring to Him. That offering is Jesus. When we chose to live a life through Jesus the ultimate sacrifice, God is pleasantly pleased with us. Jesus, the Lamb of God, is the sacrifice, and God sees the Son as perfect. There is only one way to the Father. Jesus is the path to the Father. God is looking at Jesus, not who we are or what we have done. God looks at the sacrifice that we are bringing to Him to enter into His presence. He is looking at the condition of the sacrifice not us. Jesus's condition was spotless. In the Old Testament, an animal sacrifice was brought to the altar, and the only way the sin could be forgiven was if the sacrifice was spotless. By accepting Jesus, the Lamb of God, who takes away the sins of the world, we are choosing the good way that the Lord intended for us. He knew He had to make a change because the laws could not be followed. This one-time sacrifice of Jesus Christ, the Messiah, sealed the deal (see John 1:29). A great book with more information on the kingdom, covenants, and mission of Jesus Christ is *The Apostolic Mission of Jesus the Messiah* by Gary Larson.

Jesus Christ came and carried out the glory of God. Luke 1:35 (NKJV), the most powerful moment in the Bible, states, "And the angel answered and said to her, 'The Holy Spirit will come upon you, and the power of the Highest will overshadow you; therefore, also, that Holy One who is to be born will be called the Son of God'" (Luke 1:35 NKJV).

We cannot build and expand the kingdom of God without the Holy Spirit in the body of Christ. The Holy Spirit works in the mind, body, heart, and spirit of those who believe (John 14:12–17). We need the power of God in us to fulfill the Great Commission (Matthew 28:19). When we share the good news through evangelizing, through our own testimonies or through love, we are activating the Holy Spirit within us. The power of God and His great works began to materialize in and through us. Through our commitment to Jesus, our lives become the ministry of Jesus, mirroring His image and making the world a better place. God's power reigns in and radiates out of us. He is our strength. God has given us a hunger within to want to satisfy Him (Philippians 2:13). When we accept Jesus as our

Savior, we can begin to work in our callings, fulfilling all purposes in our books written in heaven.

> *Your eyes saw my substance, being yet unformed.*
> *And in Your book they all were written,*
> *The days fashioned for me,*
> *When as yet there were none of them. (Psalm 139:16 NKJV)*

In our books, God planned our whole lives. In fact the Bible says that He knew us before we were in the womb. Before our parents even thought about us, God was thinking about us and our destinies. This is why it is so important to not veer from the good way. We must cling to what once was. We need to follow the unique patterns of the ancients.

> *Father, I come to You today and ask You to open our eyes of understanding, removing the veil for us to see the ancient paths You have set for us to follow. I ask You to show us more of You and help us to recognize the tools that You have set aside for us. I pray for Your goodness to carry us and increase our faith. May the signs and wonders that we do glorify You and influence the rest of the world. May we help You by planting seeds for the harvest. May these seeds grow in the hearts of believers and nonbelievers. May they leave a permanent marker on them. Just as You created land markers in the old days for the ancients not to sway from, Father, I pray that You create boundaries within us that make your laws written in our hearts sustain us at all times. We love You and glorify Your name. Come, Holy Spirit.*

God shared with Joel of what the future held for the church age, and this revelation became the book of Acts. We are living in the church age today. What God showed Joel and what happened in Acts came through Jesus Christ for us. God speaks to us today through His Son (Hebrews 1:1–2). These gifts are available and working today through many believers. When we receive Jesus and begin to work in the ways of the Lord instead of working in the ways of the world, an alignment occurs, and this balance restores heaven on earth. Jesus is the key to heaven on earth. The door is open through the Son. When we are in harmony with the Lord, our thoughts about who we are and whom God says we are help us to begin receiving from the Lord. The more we hunger, the more He wants to reveal to us. God fashioned us for His purpose and fulfillment (Ephesians 2:10). This synchronization occurs when we make a shift in our mindset from living according to the way of the world to being kingdom minded. This is God's intended way for us to live. We essentially are living from the vertical view. The Holy Spirit takes form, residing in us and empowering us with supernatural abilities as seen in Joel. The closer we draw near to the Father, the more we receive. It is not us but rather the Holy Spirit through us. We can do nothing without the help of the Father.

The Holy Spirit in Old Testament times was as just as alive as He is today in our hearts (see 2 Corinthians 1:22). We were made from the breath of God in His image. The same Holy Spirit who hovered over the water came upon prophets, worked through priests, and gave kings and judges dreams is alive and available to us today through Jesus Christ, the Savior of the world.

God has a place at His table for you, sons and daughters. Living a life through Christ gives us the same callings of the ancient ones who have gone before us. Jesus was a wise child full of questions. At the age of twelve, He stayed behind from his parents at the festival of the Passover. There it was in the temple that He began to learn from the teachers, gaining wisdom from the favor of His Father (Luke 2:41–52). It wasn't until he was baptized with the Holy Spirit that He began to work in the power of God. When he came out of His wilderness of testing after forty days, He began His ministry. Are you ready to begin yours?

Father, I thank You for all the revelation that You have revealed to us through this chapter. Father, I ask today that with every eye on reading these pages and every finger navigating the ancient ways of old, an outpouring of Your Spirit bursts upon the reader. I am praying for a transformation and that Your ancient ways of long ago seep deep into our hearts. I pray to get back to the ways of old, gaining clarity and a deeper revelation of who You are and who we are in You. Help us to return to You, our first love. Father, I pray that this book will help readers gain a better realization into Your inner and outer workings of them living in this world but not of this world. With every finger flipping through these Spirit-filled pages, I pray for action and big moves to take place. I pray for a deeper sense of clarity and wisdom. I pray utterances to occur and the spontaneity of Your Spirit to fill this time. Out from this filling, I pray for an overflow of Your goodness so we too can spread the good news! I pray that You touch each reader according to Your ways and that readers begin to see these kingdom paths to follow. I pray Your blessings and Your glory to be reveled through this encounter. May the readers dream dreams, see visions, and prophesy Your words. May they walk in Your ways all their days, and may their faith increase evermore as their intimacy with You also does. Thank You for using us and giving us Your Spirit to walk in Your ways as You intended. Come, Holy Spirit.

Notes

1. Nation 2 Nation Christian University, *Hebrews Chapter 9 New Covenant Worship.*
2. Larson, *The Apostolic Mission of Jesus the Messiah*

Chapter 3

Ancient Prayers: The Throne of Grace and Legalities

Pray without ceasing.
1 Thessalonians 5:17 (NKJV)

Paul the apostle was one of the ancient ones who went before us who tells us to pray without ceasing. He is telling us that our everyday conversation and intimacy with the Lord is prayer. Prayer is a gift, a two-way communication given to us to learn to know the Father in a more intimate way. This gift is a tool to be added to your tool belt to help you on your journey. By talking to God, we can ask Him things and also receive from Him. He can download His thoughts into us and can do this in numerous ways. But first we must practice the art of getting to know Him. Prayer is tapping into the heart of God, and when our hearts are aligned with His, the unthinkable takes place. We step into the supernatural realm and start living in this world but not of this world. We begin to understand who we really are through our relationship with our Father. God shows and gives according to what He knows we need. As we mature in the Father, we begin to discern the way we need to pray. The Bible, our life manual, tells us how to pray, intercede, repent, war, heal, and more. It is also full of the various ways that God speaks to us, including visions, dreams, His audible voice, prophecy, and prayer.

Jesus was a great example of praying without ceasing. He was regularly in communication with His Father. In John 5:19, He said the Son can do nothing by Himself; he can only do what he sees his Father doing, because whatever the Father does the Son does in like manner. Jesus knew that by praying, things would be revealed to Him. His two-way conversation with the Father allowed Him to move in the Spirit on earth and do the things that He was destined to do for His Father in heaven.

Prayer is a partnership, and when we co-labor with God, we are communing with Him. This friendship is what helps us to be prepared for what is happening today and what is to come. When you enter into your time alone with the Lord, start by giving Him thanks for all the things that He has done for you. Be still and allow your thoughts of thanksgiving to come forth so you can shower the Lord with praise. While you are praising Him, switch to asking Him what is on His heart. This is a good lesson on being still and pausing in the presence of the Lord. Have a Selah moment and allow God to speak to you. He will make known to you His requests. He may show you a picture, give you a vision of something, or place a word into your heart. You may want to have a journal ready to write down all the things that God shows you. He may even speak to you through praise and thanksgiving or feeling of how He loves and sees you. As He fills you with His anointing oil of the Holy Spirit, His presence overwhelms you with feelings of bliss. It may cause you to get chills at times, and at other times you may feel a feeling of electric impulses running through you making the hair on your arms rise in elation. This is your intimate time with the Father, and this is where He will reveal His heart for you. God may overwhelm your spirit with such an urgency to begin to utter words of worship to Him. You may start to sing words or songs of worship and praise as you enter deeper into His presence. Don't think about what is happening, simply move with the moment and allow the Father to take over your total being surrendering all to your Daddy. He may also share with you things that you may need to deal with. When you hear from Him, move into your own petitions for Him and be sure to thank Him for the divine appointment! The more you pray, the more your relationship with the Father deepens, and the better it gets! Spiritual alignment, discernment, wisdom, and growth rise up through prayer. Daily communion with the Father gives us the wisdom to see the tactics of the enemy. When we are in warfare, we can use all our spiritual armor of God as we battle to break supernatural strongholds and agreements of the enemy, securing our place of victory with our Father.

Weapons and Battle

We are glory carriers, and we carry the power of God wherever we go. Ephesians 6:11–12 (NKJV) tells us, "Put on the whole armor of God, that you may be able to stand against the wiles of the devil. For we do not wrestle against flesh and blood, but against principalities, against powers, against the rulers of the darkness of this age, against spiritual hosts of wickedness in the heavenly places."

Prayer is a part of the armor of God that is needed for spiritual warfare (Ephesians 6:18). Our struggle is a spiritual struggle. Prayer is our weapon, the most important tool on our belt. This piece of armor moves us into the spiritual realm along with the help of the Holy Spirit. When we pray in the armor of God, we pray in the spirit, calling on the help of the Lord. Prayer activates the rest of our spiritual armor. With the favor of prayer, we can tap into the power of God. If you want to be victorious, you need to be in communion with the Father. Just as you move throughout your day on earth, the spirit realm is at battle for your soul. The battle is real, and in the spirit realm, the enemy is working against us as we speak. He is always looking for a place of entry on us. The gift of prayer allows us to go to the Father and be able to ask Him what is on His heart, as well as what He sees that we may not see but is keeping us from being pure in heart and reaching our full potential. Prayer is a battle weapon. Scripture tells us about the power of repenting. When we go to the Father and ask Him for forgiveness, our books in heaven will be closed, allowing no access for the enemy. We can also go to the Father and intercede or stand in the gap for others just as Jesus, our Mediator, does for us. Once we close the door on the enemy, we must not look back or try to revisit what just happened. We should walk out our freedom and not put ourselves back into bondage. The enemy would love for us to do this so he can stall us.

> *The thief does not come except to steal, and to kill,*
> *and to destroy. I have come that they may have life,*
> *and that they may have it more abundantly.*
> *(John 10:10 NKJV)*

The enemy comes to destroy and wants to keep you from your destiny. Part of your destiny is receiving gifts from God to help you along the way. Vision is a gift, and along with discernment, you will also be able to help others to overcome the enemy. This is the continuation of what Jesus did, and He said we would also do greater things (John 14:12 NKJV). Vision from the Holy Spirit helps you see and understand how the enemy tries to cling to you. We need vision because the enemy is sly and will not stop trying to pull us away from the Lord. He uses many tactics such as other people and our own thoughts. Revelation says it best:

> *Then I heard in heaven, "Now salvation, and strength, and the*
> *kingdom of our God, and the power of His Christ have come,*
> *for the accuser of our brethren, who accuses them before our God*
> *day and night, has been cast down." (Revelation 12:10 NKJV)*

In life, there will always be people who do not agree or like you. They may also gossip about you and speak words into the atmosphere against you, which helps the enemy gain legal access to you (James 3:1–12). However, there is no one who will do this twenty-four hours a day except the enemy, as stated in Revelation 12:10. This is why David prays to God in the book of Psalms to search his heart (Psalm 139:23–24). Pause here, take a moment to go into prayer, and ask the Holy Spirit if there is any stronghold working against you that is hindering you in walking out your calling. Take captive every thought you have by gaining control over any belief that is not of God for your life. Second Corinthians 10:4–6 (NKJV) tells us, "For the weapons of our warfare are not carnal but mighty in God for pulling down strongholds, casting down arguments and every high thing that exalts itself against the knowledge Of God, bringing every thought into captivity to the obedience of Christ and being ready to punish all disobedience when your obedience is fulfilled."

This hindrance may be what is trying to hold you back. Taking up the weapon of prayer by giving thanks and praise, speaking the words of God over your life, calling on the name of Jesus, and asking the Father to show you any barriers so that He can cleanse you and make your heart pure again. Because we live in a fallen world, we will need to continue to check our hearts by going to the Father and asking Him to show us any burdens that may be delaying us from Him and making our hearts unclean targets for the enemy. These impediments open doors in us that are access points to the enemy. The more time we spend with the Father, the more we will begin to know when we need to go to Him and repent to close these doors and remain pure in heart. There are many things that cause blockages with the Father; some include bitterness, anger, depression, anxiety, hatred, hurt, sickness, generational curses, witchcraft, and masonry more. None of these are of God and must go. None of these are of God or are attributes of a pure heart, and they must go. The only one who controls our hearts is our Father with the Holy Spirit through righteous, faith, love, and peace (2 Timothy 2:22–24).

God loves you so much, and He wants you to be in alignment with Him according to how He sees you. When you see yourself from any of the above aspects, you are not in alignment with the Lord. From time to time, we all fall under some of these categories. The key is to be able to recognize this and to know what to do when the enemy comes creeping. This is where we need prayer and repentance most of all. It is through our relationship with the Lord that we learn to be like Him and operate as heirs of our King. It may be time to check yourself and evaluate your status of how you see yourself. Your lens may need adjusted so you can see who you are and the way God sees you. Only then can you wage war with prayer and battle against the enemy, being victorious with God by your side.

Father, I come to You today and ask You to open our spiritual eyes and senses. I ask You, Father, to make us sensitive to our surroundings, to be led by the Holy Spirit and the Spirit of Truth through our prayer time with You. Father, give us new ways to think and mature our thoughts of understanding by giving us wisdom to know. Make us mighty warriors in you, our great King! Let every thought or word coming out of us be perceived of Your words and perception. I ask You, Lord, to show us if there are any strongholds working against us that we may repent and break agreements, so that we may continue to walk out our destiny in You. Thank You, Father. We love You. Come, Holy Spirit

When we move in our gifting's that God has given to us by co-laboring with God through prayer and our alignment with Him, our books are opened, and we begin to move in our destiny. Our books were created before we were even thought of. Just as the ones who followed the ancient paths had callings, so do we (Psalm 139:15–17 NKJV; 2 Timothy 1:9 NKJV).

Ancient Paths

Your eyes saw my substance, being yet unformed.
And in Your book, they all were written, The days
Fashioned for me, When as yet there none of them.
(Psalm 139:16 NKJV)

When we pray to God, we are moving and shifting the atmosphere. When we are in alignment with the Father, then all that we do is for the glory of His kingdom. We need to know God and have a relationship with Him to live out our lives for Him. Without a relationship with the Lord, we won't know our part. Prayer is the switch.

Ephesians 1 talks about being predestined; this means our predetermined outcome or potential. It is our choice regarding what we do with what God has written in our books. He has given us free will because He loves us and wants us to want Him as helpers. He wants us to come to Him so that we will never thirst again. Only He can give us what we feel is missing. Nothing can take the place of what our Father has for us. There is one against us who is trying to delay our time, and that is why it is crucial to follow 1 Thessalonians 5:17 and pray without ceasing. The enemy does not want us to fulfill our destiny. He would rather see us living the usual mundane life than grow and mature in the Father. An example of how the enemy tries to attack us and delay us is seen in Job 1:6–12. God knew that Job was consistent in his prayer life, so He allowed Satan to test him. We must remind ourselves daily who our God is. When the enemy comes to steal, rob, and kill, we will recognize the nature of the battle and will not be deceived (Psalm 46:1 TPT; Psalm 23:4 TPT). Anytime that we shift the atmosphere by walking out our kingdom destinies, there will be a battle. Are you prepared? Fix your eyes on the Lord (Hebrews 12:1–2 TPT). There are many more stories in the Bible of how the enemy is scheming. He is doing this today as we speak, but we have a great weapon. The weapon of prayer takes us directly to the Father, and He fights with us and for us.

Thank You, Father, for showing us where we may have fallen short. For we know that Your hand is on us and that You go before us. We know that You have prepared a way for us before we were in the womb. We come to You now in the name of Your Son, Jesus Christ. We repent for the ways that we see ourselves and ask for Your forgiveness. Your Word tells us how You see us, and we ask forgiveness for allowing the enemy to get into our thoughts, shifting who we truly are and how you see us. We also ask You to show us any other area that we may need to repent or may be holding us back from our destinies. Moreover, we ask You for forgiveness. We plead the blood of Your Son, Jesus Christ, over us and ask that our books in heaven be closed so that the enemy has no legal access to us. We thank You, Father, for You are so good, and we love You so much. Come, Holy Spirit

The Throne of Grace and the Blood of Sprinkling

Throughout the scriptures, we are taught how to grasp what is available to us through the power of prayer. Some scriptures you may be already know; for example, in Matthew 7:7, God is telling us to ask, seek, and knock. But did you know that hidden throughout the Bible, there are ways to war and to defeat the enemy? Did you know that we have access to the Throne of Grace?

Let us therefore come boldly to the throne of grace that we may obtain mercy and find grace to help in time of need.
(Hebrews 4:16 NKJV)

This verse is telling us that when we go to the throne of grace, we can find mercy and grace. The throne of grace is a place in the heavenly realm that functions as a judiciary setting. When we go into prayer, we can picture ourselves going directly into the courtroom and presenting our case of what is on our heart. The courtroom is full of counsel including, Jesus, our mediator; Satan, the accuser; and God, our great Judge. The Bible is full of legal jargon. Daniel 7 is filled with courtroom proceedings. Daniel had a dream, and in that dream he had a vision of these proceedings.

> *I watched until thrones were put in place, and the Ancient of Days was seated; His garment was as white as snow, the hair of His head was like pure wool. His throne was a fiery flame, Its wheels a burning fire; A fiery stream issued and came forth from before Him. A thousand thousands ministered to Him; Ten thousand times Ten thousand stood before Him. The court was seated, And the books were opened.*
> *(Daniel 7:9–10 NKJV)*

This vision that Daniel experienced is a picture of our glorious King, the Judge, sitting on the throne of judgment. We too have access to make petitions, and through prayer we stand before the great Judge. Through appealing, we can go into the courtroom and approach our Father, the mighty Judge, and plead our case. We can also go in for other people and intercede. This is why prayer is so important. Prayer is a gift given to each believer to be used as a weapon and to move in the supernatural ways of the kingdom of God. The ancient ones who have gone before us have opened this door of opportunity for us to also receive this gift. John 15:15 (NKJV) tells us, "No longer do I call you servants, for a servant does not know what his master is doing; but I have called you friends, for all things that I heard from My Father I have made known to you."

Now that we are friends of God, He reveals to us more of who He is and His greatness. We now have eyes to see through His Spirit. With these new eyes, we can see into what scripture is telling us as we read the Word of God (Matthew 13:11). The Word of God instructs us and shows us passages about His courts, the throne of grace, the power and authority we have in Him, and how to access these things. Through reading His Spirit-filled pages, more is revealed to us. When we pray, our spirits go to the Father to connect with Him and an exchange occurs. Not all prayers require us to go into the legal system of heaven, but they many have spiritual root forces of all kinds that need to be dealt with from a court case aspect. Some of these prayers include sickness, depression, substance abuse, rejection, bitterness, anger, disorders, our own thoughts and words, generational curses, witchcraft, and masonry. These are the roots that put us into battle mode. By talking to the Father, we will learn to hear Him. By following the ancient paths of those in the Bible who went before us, and through studying scripture, we will learn how to pray as things come up.

What a gift the throne of grace is! In this world today, it is easy to get off course, just as we read of so many ancient ones throughout the Bible have done. Just as they were called into the kingdom of God, so are we! Through Jesus Christ, the Savior for the world, we have access directly to God. The throne of grace is given to us to restore our hearts and set the foundation of the world on the axis that God intended. When we move in sync with Him, a supernatural shift occurs, and we begin to move in victory after victory for the Lord. Jesus made a way for us. God prepared the way before we were thought of and He had a plan. Through His Son, we are able to be heirs of the kingdom of God. Through following after the ways of Jesus's life on earth, we create heaven on earth. We are walking out the plans of the Great Architect! The Lord is with us continually and never leaves us (Joshua 1:9; Matthew 28:20). It is we who veer with voided vision at times. The throne of grace gives us the opportunity to make petitions, asking the Father what needs to be expelled from us or from others. God is our weapon against the dark forces of the enemy. When we come forth and boldly ask the Father what it is that needs released, we can move into breaking all agreements with the things that the enemy has attached to us. Then through asking for forgiveness, pleading the blood of Jesus over us, and the situation, we are restored. *Operating in the Courts of Heaven* by Robert Henderson is a great book that goes more in-depth on this subject.

Blood of Sprinkling

In the Old Testament, blood sacrifices were meant to establish foundations for forgiveness. They brought hope to believers while bringing them back into accord with God. This atonement made it possible for favor of the Lord to be obtained. This was, a fundamental rule or way of obtaining mercy and grace—from Genesis, when the sacrifice was one lamb for one man; through Exodus, when it was one lamb for one house onward; to Leviticus, when it was one lamb for one nation; and lastly to Jesus, who was one Lamb for one world (Genesis 3,4; Exodus 12:3; Leviticus 23:18–19, 27–28; John 3:16).

In Exodus 24:4–8 (NKJV), Moses sprinkled blood as part of the observance to the covenant or promise of the Israelites. The sprinkling of blood is a testimony for repentance. Today, our redemption comes by the blood of Jesus Christ, the Savior of the world! Yes, the blood of Jesus Christ stopped the enemy in his tracks! If only the enemy would have known, he would have thought twice before sending Jesus to the cross. This is the greatness of our God. He is all-powerful and all-knowing. He knew what He had to do, and through the sacrifice of His Son, we now are free and can begin to walk out our destinies. We now will do greater things for the kingdom of God (John 14:12)! Only the blood of Jesus Christ can take away our sins. This is the key to our faith.

> *But He was wounded for our transgressions,*
> *He was bruised for our iniquities;*
> *The chastisement for our peace was upon Him,*
> *And by His stripes we are healed. (Isaiah 53:5 NKJV)*

The animal blood covered the sins of those under the old covenant. The blood of Jesus Christ was a one-time ultimate sacrifice washing away all the sins of both the Old and New Testament people. The laws set forth in the old covenant were ways of following God that could not be realized. They failed again and again, but

Jesus in our hearts is not temporary—He is forever. He makes it possible for us to go directly to the Lord whenever we need anything. Jesus gave righteousness to us when He redeemed us on the cross. God is a living, functioning part in us, and through His grace and mercy, we can be forgiven. Through this, much was given to us, and now we must move forth to carry the ministry of Jesus with us daily.

Jesus was the final sacrifice, a one-stop shop, giving us redemption and making us righteous. It is through His mercy and grace that our union is complete in Him and that we receive the gift of the Holy Spirit in us. The old covenant came through Moses, and the new covenant came through Jesus. We needed the old to get the new! He is the heir of all things (Hebrews 1:1–2).

When we go into the court of heaven, to the throne of grace, we plead the blood of Jesus over the case after we petition and repent for the sins of the case that has been established. The blood of Jesus Christ cleanses the sins, and then we can ask for our books to be closed, leaving no legal access for the enemy. Breakthrough takes place in the courts of heaven. Jesus's blood is powerful! Come into agreement with the blood of Jesus when you enter the throne of grace. Redemption comes from our agreement with the blood of Jesus. Jesus's blood has a voice, and that voice is the reason He came to earth. He shed His blood to give us life. He is our salvation (Isaiah 49:6)! I mentioned earlier that if you would like more reading on this matter, Robert Henderson's book *Operating in the Courts of Heaven* is full of insight.

> *"Come now, and let us reason together," Says the Lord,*
> *"Though your sins are like scarlet, They shall be as white as snow;*
> *Though they are red like crimson, They shall be as wool."*
> *(Isaiah 1:18 NKJV)*

A pure heart lives in hideaway with the Father. He is our protector. Whatever it is that we experience, God wants to be a part of it. He is our helper. He created us to be weaker to want Him to aid and guide us. We are never alone and can do nothing on our own. The Holy Spirit lives in and through us. Understanding our identity in Christ is crucial. It helps us in knowing who we are and how powerful we are when we go into prayer with the Father. When we speak and ask of the Lord, the Ancient of Days responds in favor and joy that we have come to Him! This friendship we have with the Lord keeps us in tune with Him, and His Spirit guides us along the way. Pray with me from Psalm 91 (NKJV).

He who dwells in the secret place of the Most High Shall abide under the shadow of the Almighty. I will say of the Lord, "He is my refuge and my fortress; My God, in Him I will trust." Surely He shall deliver you from the snare of the fowler And from the perilous pestilence. He shall cover you with His feathers, And under His wings you shall take refuge; His truth shall be your shield and buckler. You shall not be afraid of the terror by night, Nor of the arrow that flies by day, Nor of the pestilence that walks in darkness, Nor of the destruction that lays waste at noonday. A thousand may fall at your side, And ten thousand at your right hand; But it shall not come near you. Only with your eyes shall you look, And see the reward of the wicked. Because you have made the Lord, who is my refuge, Even the Most High, your dwelling place, No evil shall befall you, Nor shall any plague come near your dwelling; For He shall give His angels charge over you, To keep you in all your ways. In their hands they shall bear you up, Lest you dash your foot against a stone. You shall tread upon the lion and the cobra, The young lion and the serpent you shall trample underfoot. "Because he has set his love upon Me, therefore I will deliver him; I will set him on high, because he has known My name. He shall call upon Me, and I will answer him; I will be with him in trouble; I will deliver him and honor him. With long life I will satisfy him, And show him My salvation."

God has not given a spirit of fear when we are facing attacks from the enemy. He has given us His love and power! Set your eyes on the Lord, your rock and firm foundation. Search the scriptures for God's promises for you. Meditate on the Word of God and let it soak into your being like a sponge. Let Him fill you up with His presence!

Let us draw near with a true heart in full assurance of faith,
having our hearts sprinkled from an evil conscience
and our bodies washed with pure water.
(Hebrews 10:22 NKJV)

A sign of true worship! The way we draw near to God is through having pure hearts and being faithful, our bodies washed in the Word and our hearts sprinkled from evil conscience.

Search me, O God, and know my heart;
Try me, and know my anxieties;
And see if there is any wicked way in me,
And lead me in the way everlasting.
(Psalm 139:23–24 NKJV)

I love Psalm 139. David asks God to search his heart. He is saying, "Search all of me. I give you all of me to comb through. I completely surrender to you. If I have any wickedness in me, remove it from me because I only want to walk Your way." Wickedness comes in many forms. We may think we are good people because we go to church every Sunday, tithe; serve in the community, and more. But if we have any idols of any sorts, then they are not of God. [1]Idols come in many forms. *Merriam-Webster*'s definition of an idol is anything that we do in extreme devotion, a likeness of something. An idol is anything that we get to focused on that takes away our focus of God. Worry, bitterness, anger, and more are just a few to name. It may also be our reoccurring thoughts. When we

---

[1] Merriam-Webster, s.v. "idol (n.)," accessed April 13, 2021, https://www.merriam-webster.com/dictionary/idol. Merriam-Webster's definition of an idol is anything that we do in extreme devotion, a likeness of something.

take matters in our own hands, we often get stuck. We lose focus on God, our provider who makes all things new. David is saying, "Take all of me and search me out. Tell me where I may have taken a wrong turn from You, my King. I don't want to walk along the wrong path. I want to tread upon Your path, the ancient way. For You are the Ancient of Days who knows all my thoughts before they are even thought of."

When we draw near to God in the Hebrews 10:22 way, using the same prayer that David prayed for our own lives, God will show us where we may have fallen short, and we will know the things for which we need to repent. After God shows us the areas we need to ask for forgiveness for, we need to go to Him in prayer at the throne of grace, repenting and breaking all agreements that we have made with the enemy. When we pray, we are praying from the natural into the spiritual realm because God is of Spirit. These things that are revealed to us by God that are not of Him, can only be from another source—the enemy, who comes to steel, rob, and kill. Sometimes we do not even know that we are forming spiritual agreements such as these until we get stuck and stop seeing any breakthroughs in our lives. We are good people, but we must understand that the enemy is sly and will try anything to keep us from the will of God and His purposes for our lives. By going to God through David's way and asking Him to show us these agreements that we have unknowingly formed, we can get to the solution. We can ask for forgiveness, break the agreements with the enemy, plead the blood of Jesus over us, and then ask our Father to close our books in heaven. When we walk out of prayer, we walk out in faith, not looking back but forward. God tells us in Matthew 7:7–8 that when we ask for something, it will be given to us. The roots of those agreements are no longer in business. They cannot consume us anymore. Now, our walk once again looks more like our Father's walk along the ancient path.

Our prayers work! They remove obstacles and stop the enemy from pulling us down. Throughout life, we will need to go to the courts of heaven many times, disputing our cases that have been brought against from the enemy. God is so good and takes care of His children. He hears our prayers. He has given us this gift of being able to go directly to Him through His Son, Jesus Christ, whose blood makes us clean. He purifies us making us look more like Him. The blood of the Son takes away our sins. Whenever we need a breakthrough, we can go directly to the Lord to regain our purity and cleanliness, to continue fulfilling the callings that God has bestowed upon our lives. Our Father is always ready to release goodness to His children! The good news is that we can also do this for others too. Our bold prayers hit the spiritual realm and shift all the doings of the enemy. Thank You, Father, for the uncontainable love that You have for us!

Father, we love You so much. Thank You for bringing a refreshment to our spirit. Thank You for always coming through and providing the things that we cannot get on our own. Father, we need You in our lives every moment we tread these ancient paths. We are so thankful for Your Word that You give us to use as a tool to know You more and to learn to walk in a deeper intimacy with You. Everything You give us in the Bible is for us, and we thank You for opening it to us the further we dig into it. It is the greatest tangible item You have left us on this earth. Thank You for providing us direct access to You through Your Son. Father, just to think about what Jesus went through breaks us. We owe You our lives. Nothing compares to His act of saving us, to live. We will be good stewards of the gifts You give, and we will walk them out. We also want to thank You for teaching us how to pray specifically for anything that is not of You and to pray and intercede for others in need. Thank You for giving us strength just as You sent an angel form heaven to give strength to Jesus in His time of anguish in the Garden of Gethsemane. Thank You for always being forgiving through Your grace and mercy. Thank You for the new covenant, being written on our hearts and being able to go to You directly to receive purification. Thank You for showing us how your judicial system in heaven works, and thank You for

opening our eyes of understanding and our ears of enlightenment
to work in Your ways. Father, we ask You today to show us more
of who You are and to bring us into fullness through the process
of maturation as we learn Your doings. Thank You for entrusting
us to carry out Your purposes for the world! Come, Holy Spirit.

Notes

1. Robert Henderson, *Operating in the Courts of Heaven,* Robert Henderson Ministries, 2014
2. Nation 2 Nation Christian University, "The Epistle to the Hebrews," session 1, page 3, section H.

Chapter 4

Ancient Days of Fasting

"Now, therefore," says the Lord,
"Turn to Me with all your heart,
With fasting, with weeping, and with mourning."
—Joel 2:12 (NKJV)

Fasting is part of God's design for us. It is an action taken to draw closer to the Lord. Actions make way for change, which is what the ancients were often in need of due to choices made based on their own perception. Just as the ways of old, we too make choices and often get stuck in the ways of the world requiring a shift to occur. The ancient cultures that went before us left us the blueprint for fasting to attain spiritual direction and dependence on God. Throughout history and over many generations, fasting was sometimes required for healing, discretion, restoration, or mourning, or to humble oneself. Fasting sometimes also resulted in dreams and visions. We fast for many reasons. We fast when we are looking for solutions to problems; for spiritual growth; to draw near to God; for revival, devotion, worship, freedom of bondage, healing for the world, or hunger; to lift burdens; and more. Just like those of old who struggled, we still struggle today. This ancient practice is a sign of hope. Through restoration, adoration, and dedication of oneself to the will of God, or to hear God's voice, breakthrough occurs through fasting. Many times you will see this in the Bible during moments of destruction. Abstaining from something and replacing it with prayers, along with praise and worship, will result in the realignment of ourselves with the Father. When we are working in perfect harmony, balanced and in sync with the Lord, we begin to move in mirror image of Jesus doing the will of God. Denying ourselves for the glory of God will take us to another level, such as reigning from the kingdom of God and putting us in a place of favor. In 2 Chronicles 20:3, Jehoshaphat announced a fast for all of Judah. He sought the Lord out in fear of being attacked. The Lord came upon a Levite, telling him to relay a message: not to be afraid but to stand firm and watch the deliverance from the Lord. The Lord was with them. When we are seeking God in thanksgiving and praise, we seal the guarantee of God. God delivers us in our loyalty to Him.

The ancient path of fasting has been lost to humanity for some time. The ways of the world, along with "New Age" ideas, have taken over, and this new transfer of focus has been identified and demonstrated as the "new" materialistic course of humankind. Earthly idolatry has taken away the will and purpose of God. Many have regressed in the God-given inheritance that the Lord has purposed for them. God never changes. His ways have been set and put into place for what kingdom living looks like in the blueprint of the creation of the world. This ancient document provided and established an ideal, unique pattern of our lives' purpose. When we veer away from God and create our own truths of what is real, what is right and wrong, we get off the ancient paths and follow the path of the earthly world without the will of God, forgetting to whom we belong. Too often we rely on worldly truths. Just as generations before us relied on the Farmer's Almanac for answers to everyday things in preparation for the day, today we rely on things such as Google. Google is a convenient collection of one's opinionated news, because everyone has a version of truth, and it's hard to tell what is truth.

The hope we have for today and for future generations is to reference the ancient truths of the Ancient of Days, God Himself. The Word defines truth and is the singular reference point to anything else that determines whether it is truth. The Ancient of Days is calling us back to Him. By taking actions of self-denial and surrendering in complete devotion to the Lord through repentance, prayer, and fasting, we will be reestablished into our rightful place within the dominion of God. We were never meant to live the world's truths by overruling or stepping over our boundaries of God's blueprint. We were created to co-labor with Him depending on Him, receiving and releasing the everlasting deity of God.

Many ancients who have gone before us have fallen and then returned to the Lord, receiving the long-suffering mercies of the Lord. Manasseh is one of them. God delivered Him (2 Chronicles 33:12–13). These ancient paths have not changed direction; we have. Our eyes have set themselves among men, and our thoughts have been reprogrammed into seeing what temporarily fills us rather than being permanently filled with the love of God. When we follow God's master plan for our lives, only then will our eyes be rebirthed bringing us into complete deliverance. With these new eyes comes new vision. Our present perception comes from the binocular standpoint, where we are seeing with the eyes of Jesus. Our new view will show us these ancient paths. As we set our feet upon the narrow pathways, we pursue the same unique patterns of those who made their lives a mirror image of God. Choosing to stand bold, we will walk in confidence of the ancients who paved the way for us. One day we too will leave our footprints on these ancient paths for generations to come. The everlasting filling of the Lord brings about an outpouring and overflow that is then released into the atmosphere; touching others and making us thirst no more. This new focal point moves us into our true inheritance given to us from the Father. Fasting shows us the true meaning of surrendering to see that we were placed here for the purpose of God to move and live in union with Him. When we turn from God, our ways turn to idols of all types of things that are not of God, and the truth becomes distorted. When a human's hands get involved, the kingdom comes crashing down. We must remember who we are and to whom we belong. Fasting along with prayer brings us back into alignment with the Father. We must check our tool belt, look at our weaponry given to us from God, and start using it. We carry the power of the Holy Spirit within us; we are heirs to the throne.

As we embark on these ancient paths, giving ourselves to Him, His ways become our ways, and we begin to produce the fruit of our labor. By walking in sensitivity to the Lord and giving and receiving from each other in tandem, just as the Father is in alignment with the Son, our true identity is unveiled. When we choose to stray from the ancient ways, we depart from God and begin to walk in the truth of the world. God's truth then gets lost to what we believe is right or wrong, showing us that our free will is not always a good thing. God has given us free will because he wants us to freely come to Him through His Son. He wants us to make the unconditional choice to reign with Him, helping to provide balance while in alignment with Him, for His purposes. When we incorporate fasting and prayer within our lives, it gives us the opportunity to make amends and come back to the Lord with all our hearts. He is the great Restorer, and it is He who gives mercy and grace. Jesus Christ redeemed us, and through redemption we are made righteous.

In this new era, the time has come to take our seats in the heavenlies and begin operating in the intended ways of the ancient blueprints. It is time to acknowledge the given power and authority within us, given by God and worked out through the Holy Spirit. It is time to learn to love, time to war and be loosed from the enemy, breaking agreements and elemental worldly foundations of enslavement through the dark powers and principalities within the earth. Today is the day to move in victory with our Father as His children! The hour has come to rise and see the scope of the world through the eyes of God with the utterance of Him in us, moving forward and reigning from a heaven perspective while living on earth.

Fasting sets us back into motion on the ancient paths of those who have gone before us, providing us with a paradigm reset. A newfound strength grows and multiplies when we tread upon these age-old pathways. God is calling us to return to Him. We have followed our own ways for so long throughout history unto the present day, beginning with the Canaanites and their god Baal. We need to get back to the original design that God has for us. Fasting give us an advantage, putting us on the intended course of action for our lives so we can prepare for our ultimate future of reigning with the Lord. When we learn to reign in the kingdom of God through reading the Bible, we are activating the ancient ways of the wise throughout the ages. All scripture points to Jesus, and we read it as a whole to encompass and receive impartation from the ways of old. We are not merely reading scripture to obtain knowledge to understand the details. We read the words of God inspired through the Holy Spirit openly to receive what He has for us. We reflect on these Spirit-filled pages to focus on what God is saying to the people. We are the continuation of what started long before we were even thought of. When we recognize the patterns throughout scripture of the ways of old, we can establish these ways and move in harmony with the Ancient of Days! God wants restoration of His people. He wants recovery. He is the great Deliverer. Therefore when we submit to Him and His will through repentance and exposing the lies of the enemy, while pleading the blood of Jesus over our circumstances, He forgives us, and through our restitution with our Father, we are reestablished. Our case has been won! We are victorious with God! He closes all legal access points, and our books are closed. Now we are ready for action, moving forward in the callings of the Lord. God is simple and makes it easy for us to come to Him. The chaotic world has changed our vision to relying on the ways of the world. We tend to go to other people and other things, leaving God behind in the shadows. We have broken His heart time and time again. We have also been the cause of His fury throughout time by creating our own truths. Getting back to the ancient ways reaffirms our place with

God. Fasting is a way to learn and discern the difference between what is earthly and heavenly. The key is to make our core focus the center of God's attention, leaning not on our own understanding, looking to worldly idols for vision but surrendering in complete submission to the will of God. Fasting is just one of the many ways we have discussed in this book to draw near to God. Returning to our first love and giving Him the first hour of our day increases God's favor upon our lives. He will intimately show us who He is and the one true Way.

Father, we pray for sensitivity to Your Spirit and never swaying from Your teaching or ways. We pray for alertness and a sound-minded spiritual awakening after Your heart. We ask for clarity, vision, and ancient paths to open and to become clear, giving us the binocular vision of Jesus. Bring forth restoration and newfound gifts to boldly take our stance while walking out from this time of self-denial into our true identity within You. We pray for guidance and intuition to arise, causing a paradigm shift from the worldly ways back to the ancient way of Your blueprints. We ask for You to unveil all to us, bringing us into favor with You and Your glory. We sincerely urge You, Father, to create a hunger within the world to bring about the return of the ancient ways of fasting leaving renewed purified cleansed hearts. Father, we ask for action to take place and for assurance of every reader whose eyes glare upon these pages. We ask for knowledge and senses to be awakened spiritually and for tools to be revealed in our tool belts to move in all Your ways for Your kingdom. We pray for conquerors to come forth, as well as generals, watchmen, and prophets, and for all Your children to return to You with all their hearts. With this return, we petition for new attitudes to spring forth as your extravagant love envelopes over us to see and taste Your goodness. We pray that the practice of fasting becomes a habit in our hearts and reveals lives in action being restored and functioning in perfect harmony with You, our King! We pray for new positions to be released and for the reader to boldly receive these assignments,

*walking them out and reflecting Your goodness. Thank You for
giving us the gift of fasting, bringing our focus back on You and Your
truths. Thank You for manifesting Your presence in and through us,
causing us to shine as lights that brighten these ancient paths. Thank
You for miraculous healings, answers to our fasting prayers, clarity,
guidance, and breaking the chains of the enemy. Finally, Father,
thank You for loving us unconditionally and teaching us Your ways,
building our faith and patience while giving us strength in hope.
May You receive all the glory forever and ever. Come, Holy Spirit*

Fasting throughout Scripture

There are many documented fasts throughout the Bible but with
one theme and purpose—namely, to meditate on God. Some of
these fasts include the Ester Fast, the Daniel fast, the Ezra fast, the
Elijah fast, the Samuel fast, the Paul fast, the widows fast, the John
the Baptist fast, the disciples fast, and the Jesus fast. Within each
fast, you will recognize why the fast was introduced, and by looking
at the context along with observing the events, you will understand
why each fast occurred. We can also look at different ancients who
have gone before us and see their unique experiences of self-denial
and how it changed many outcomes. For some, the change came
internally, whereas other fasts changed groups of people in nations.
A couple changed the history of the world, as seen in the book of
Ester (4:16) and Jonah (3:5). You may also want to take a look of
how Moses, David, Ahab, Nehemiah, Cornelius, and the Israelites
fasted at different times. In all circumstances, fasting is a way to
honor God by returning back to our first love with a pure heart. Our
roots are connected to the spiritual realm of the kingdom of God.
We are spiritual beings, and fasting is a way to set the human self
aside and experience God in total surrender. God restores us when
we come to Him for help.

Let's explore some of these age-old ways of fasting laid out in the Bible and learn how we too can humbly submit ourselves to the Lord.

Go, gather together all the Jews who are in Susa, and fast for me. Do not eat or drink for three days, night or day. I and my attendants will fast as you do. When this is done, I will go to the king, even though it is against the law. And if I perish, I perish. (Esther 4:16 NIV)

In this fallen world, we will experience various trials and tribulations. Before you begin this fast, think about the root of the problem you are experiencing. The Holy Spirit has led you to this fast because of the type of feelings that you may be struggling with. You may be noticing a spiritual attack that is physically or mentally affecting you. This affliction can be on a personal level or be from world. Keep in mind that we are told in Ephesians 6:12 that we do not wrestle against flesh and blood but against spiritual rulers of the darkness. The good news is that the Esther fast can be used in this battle as a weapon against the enemy. The nation of Persia became a nation that acquired favor from God through fasting and prayer. Come to the Father, the Ultimate Authority who protects you. His armor shields you. As you fiercely pray for protection, stay faithful to God and remember you cannot rely on yourself. Enter His courts and receive from the Lord. It is by the power of God that He will abolish the ways of the enemy and make a way for rescue! When we fast the Esther way, we are fasting for God's divine protection from the strongholds from the enemy.

Esther was a Jewish queen famous for saving her people by exposing Haman's conspiracy to murder them. Esther called for a three-day fast, abstaining from eating or drinking day and night. When she heard of the works of Haman, the evil prince, and what he had in place, Esther fasted with her people. After three days, she boldly went to the king, exposing her religion to save her people while also risking her own life. Because she first went to the Lord and fully submitted to Him with her people, the Lord delivered her and her people (Esther 5:2). Queen Esther is a picture of bold faith, risking all to do the will of God. This is a story that inspires us to be more like Esther and Mordecai, walking courageously by faith and not sight while rising to the call of the Lord. God knows our deepest desires and wishes to make them come true. We must first submit to the will of God, coming to Him to fight the battle for us. When our focus is on the Lord and not daily distractions, God will expose the problem and will help us overcome. Discipline through fasting helps us to stay connected to the Father.

> *Please test your servants for ten days, and let them give us vegetables to eat and water to drink. (Daniel 1:12 NKJV)*

Daniel was taken into captivity as a young man after King Nebuchadnezzar attacked and took over Jerusalem. His new home was among the Babylonians. Daniel had to learn the new customs of the Babylonian pagan ways. Although Daniel was given a new name, a new language, and an entirely new culture, he never forgot to whom he belonged. He never acclimated to the ways of these people, who did not follow God. Daniel was known for his courage and strength while continuing to honor God. His strength came from the Lord, who dwelled with Daniel and spoke through him. Daniel is a role model of how to live in a Godless culture while remaining connected fully to God. Think about how hard this was for so many back then and today. When the natural eye sees what everyone else is doing while being immersed in a Godless culture for so long, many may succumb to it. Daniel never forgot with whom he dwelt. He was full of discernment and was not swayed. We live in a world today full of good and bad; God left us His Word and many gifts that go along with it to sustain us while we are here. As believers, His presence goes with us and is in us. We must not forget the ways of the old in such times. When we follow after the heart of God, we can be in any season or circumstance in life, good or bad and know the one True Way.

Daniel was a prophet who was given visions of the future by God regarding forthcoming events. God's favor was on Daniel giving him knowledge and wisdom. The faithfulness of Daniel gave him the ability to co-labor with the Father. These supernatural abilities were given by God to translate visions and dreams for the entire world. Daniel denied himself of the cultural dietary habits of the king. He refused to eat the special diet that the king had for the young men. He refrained from all food except for vegetables and water, to remain healthy and to be able to hear from God for His purposes. In secrecy, Daniel asked the steward to test him and his friends for ten days in his proposed dietary plan. At the end of the ten days after consuming only vegetables and water, the steward saw that Daniel and his friends looked healthier than most of the young who ate of the portion of food given by the king. The test that Daniel proposed was a fast. When Daniel and his friends were brought to King Nebuchadnezzar, the king found that there were no young men who even measured up to the appearance of Daniel and his friends or his requirements. Daniel and his friends found favor in the king. God prepared the way for all these workings. It was Daniel's unshaken faith in God that brought divine revelation into the natural realm and also what the future of Daniel would eventually hold for the working of God. The same spiritual abilities that God gave Daniel and his friends are available to us today. As believers, we have these abilities, but we must act in faith putting these abilities to use through humbly submitting and surrendering to the Lord. Daniel turned to the Lord through fasting and prayer. If you are in need of restoration of any kind, the Daniel fast is a good fast to cleanse the body and restore health. Through fasting and prayer, breakthrough occurs, and the will of God is made known (Daniel 1:5–21, 10:3).

As we can see, there are many ancients who have fasted to hear from God throughout the ages. The key is to humbly come before God while consecrating and denying oneself to focus on God and receive from Him. The way we fast can look different according to one's health or intentions. Assuming you have no underlying health issues that prevent fasting, abstaining from something that is consumed on a daily basis can bring inner healing and restoration. Fasting can look like abstaining from food and water, skipping a meal, giving up something good, or refraining from consuming meat and replacing it with vegetables. It can be a full-on fast, a partial fast, an intermittent fast, or a rotating fast. I have found that *Fasting for Spiritual Breakthrough* by Elmer L. Towns is great book with in-depth detail of the many different types of fasting. Only you will know the burden placed upon you from God. Through prayer and supplication, the Holy Spirit will reveal the fast that is right for you.

> *He has made everything beautiful in its time. He has also set eternity in the human heart; yet no one can fathom what God has done from beginning to end. (Ecclesiastes 3:11 NIV)*

No matter whether we are fasting for preparation, forgiveness, guidance, faith, aid, sorrow, or blessing; to hear the Lord; or to wage war against the enemy, God is the great Restorer. He sets our paths straight. He acknowledges all our ways and determines our life purposes. God's timing is always perfect. He has strategically set His ancient ways in motion throughout history so that we would cling to Him, love Him, and be aware of future warning of the world. He has made a way for us to come to Him through His Son while having direct access to His kingdom as true sons and daughters. He knows the ways of the world, and He is our blessing, providing our true gifts to living in this world but not of it. When we fully submit to our Father, He takes care of all our needs. He is a good, good Father. We belong to Him. Fasting helps us remember who we are and whom we belong to by uncovering areas on the ancient paths that have been covered up. When we use our spiritual sense of perception through fasting, our spirits will be redirected to the purpose and will of God. Our true north is revealed through the powerful act of fasting to pursue God. This ancient path that comes in the form of exercising the presence of God in the waiting begins with our choice to follow the ways of old. The practice of fasting has been lost over the years and needs to be reintroduced to the world.

There have been many times in my life where I have been at a stalemate and in need of rescue. One time in particular was when I desperately needed to hear from the Lord. I had made a career for myself in the dental field, and while on a mission trip to Santo Domingo, Dominican Republic, I was given the opportunity to pray about a career change. This new area of opportunity would lead me into what I was most passionate about, however I had no skills or prior experience. When I returned home from the trip, I began to pray to God about this new life change that was unfolding before my eyes. I felt the sense to fast, so I began to fast the Daniel way to hear from the Father clearly and expose the direction for my destiny.

This was not an easy thing to do. I was in the dental field for eighteen years at that time. I had a routine that I had established, and I loved what I did. I love people, and in my field of expertise, I was able to work with all kinds of people while also getting to listen, talk, and share with them. I loved what I did, but deep down inside me, I knew that the mission field was where my heart was. I needed to fast to hear from God about making a complete change from my current occupation. I also realized that I was not young anymore and had responsibilities of my own. I had a growing family of six, which set me in my ways. Yes, I said it: *my* ways. When you think you have it all planned out, that's when God comes knocking at your door to open your eyes and show you that He has so much more in store.

Let me back up for a minute. When I was in high school, I loved Spanish class so much that I completed four levels of Spanish in three years with an A average. It came naturally to me. Now that I look back, I can see it was one of my gifting's from the Father. I loved it so much that it stuck with me like riding a bicycle. I knew deep down in my heart that I was meant for the world, meaning that I had a heart for Third World Spanish-speaking countries, but I had no direction or path at that time to lead me to my heart's desire. As time went by, I married and had four children, thus leading me to incorporate Spanish into my children's lives. The love of Spanish never left me but instead had a way of pressing on in my children. When I look back at this, I see the inner workings of God keeping this gift at the center focus of my attention. I was continuing to learn by teaching my children. The funny thing is that all four of them took Spanish in school and did well, and one actually picked the language up fairly easy in the same way I did. In fact when he was young, I took him for his eye examination, and when the doctor asked him what colors he saw, he answered in Spanish! I laughed so hard that day.

Anyway, back to my story. God put in my spirit the love for Spanish and for people. I was working in a field where I had that chance to see people every day, and that made me happy. I even was able to speak Spanish to some of my patients, which was a plus, but as I reflect on the events leading up to the turning point of my life that day in the Dominican Republic, I saw through fasting that God was preparing me for something more. When I fully submitted to the Lord through fasting for an answer, He showed up and directed my path. After the fast, I knew that it was time to start walking out my destiny. In life we all have choices to make. Sometimes we do not hear the still, small voice within leading us, and we make decisions based upon what we think is best for us. The gift is that God is so good that He gives us choice while still marking our path. He never gives up, and when we align ourselves with the Holy Spirit, we began to see more clearly and submit fully to the Lord. He continues to prepare us even in our own choices. Can you look back on your life and see how you made choices that eventually changed because God showed up? Can you see how, in your own choosing, God was still preparing you for what was to come?

When the fast ended, I knew that I was to take this new job in the global mission and local outreach field. In the years leading up to this event, I can see how God was preparing me in the area of Spanish and with people. I thank God for all the opportunity He has given me to learn and grow, and I continue to thank Him today for the assignment He has for me next! Fasting showed me how to listen for the will of God over my life. God showed me how to come into my divine destiny. When I began operating in my gifts in the mission field, the opportunity of showing others the Lord became infinite. My gifting's began to accelerate, and the Lord introduced me into even more new gifting's. I felt the joy and peace within my spirit when I was following after the will of God for my life. The awesome thing is that even with no prior training or experience, the Holy Spirit within showed up and supernaturally trained me! God put the love in my heart to go for it with everything I had. There was no room for the fear of what if; there was only space to walk out the call in faith and obedience.

I learned things that I thought I could not learn and do things that I had never done before. The powerful force of the Holy Spirit was at work not only in my life but also in the lives of all who were involved in this assignment. To this day, when I see some of my old friends who I worked with, they still say that everything we did was definitely a supernatural God thing. We never could have done any of what was accomplished on our own. I will never forget that part of my life. It was because I chose to set aside a period of time to fast and hear from the Lord instead of making the decision on my own. This also was a sign for me that I was maturing and learning to recognize that I am nothing without the Father, and that I cannot do anything without His presence in my life. You see, the Holy Spirit began to work in me when I became aligned with Him. When I took the "I" out of the conversation and asked God to show me what He has for me, I began to learn how to walk the ancient paths. I hope that my story inspires you to try fasting and to keep fasting as different things come up in your life or in the lives of others. May God guide you, shelter you, and give you the courage to walk as the ancient ones who have gone before you.

Father, we humbly come to You today in response to fasting. We know that it is hard to resist and give things up, and we ask You today to be our guide as we surrender fully to You and Your purposes. Many have come and gone who have treaded upon the ancient paths that we see as confirmations to who You are and Your goodness. We thank You for leaving these old ways for us to see Your intentions and to keep our focus on You in all times. Father, we ask that through our supplication to You, You reveal the right fast that has been uniquely authorized by You for us individually. We ask You to place it upon our hearts as a burden. We know that we will come out of this time of self-denial being made new in You. We are confident that You will reveal our hearts and full intentions through revelation to the path we are on and set us into motion on Your predetermined path for us that is written in our books. We know you will restore our petitions while bringing forth a new area of growth and opportunity within us. Father, we ask You to show us more of who You are, and we yearn to carry Your glory within us for all to see. We thank You for making us vessels for Your desires. We thank You for the day You have given us, and may we use these days of fasting in accordance to Your plans. May our destinies be released from our books in heaven, and may we take action that is revealed by the Holy Spirit within us. Come, Holy Spirit.

Notes

1. *Fasting for Spiritual Breakthrough* Elmer L. Towns, Ontario: Regal Books 1979

Chapter 5

Ancient Training:
Seeing with Spiritual Eyes

And when the servant of the man of God arose early and went out,
there was an army, surrounding the city with horses and chariots.
And his servant said to him, "Alas, my master! What shall we do?"

So he answered, "Do not fear, for those who are with us are
more than those who are with them." And Elisha prayed, and
said, "Lord, I pray, open his eyes that he may see." Then the Lord
opened the eyes of the young man, and he saw. And behold, the
mountain was full of horses and chariots of fire all around Elisha.
(2Kings 6:15-17 NKJV)

In the moment that followed Elisha's prayer to God, his servant
began to see what was unseen in the seen. The Father enlightened the
servant's eyes of understanding, and the truth was revealed. It was
by the divine knowledge and faith of Elisha that he petitioned the
Father in prayer to take away the servant's fear. Elisha fully trusted
in God regardless of what was to come, and therefore he fearlessly
declared to the Lord to open his servant's eyes.

When the eyes of our understanding are opened, we begin to see God at work in our lives as our fears diminish and our faith increases. The story of Elisha and his servant is a great story of following ancient paths. Moving from fear to faith causes activation to occur. When we follow Jesus, His twelve disciples, the Old Testament prophets, and modern disciples who have also followed the ways of our Lord, a stirring within us starts to occur. We shift from the normal, everyday living and begin to seek what those of old had. We too begin to want what was obtainable to them. Yes, you too can have all of what they had in the ancient days! Many prophets of our time also displayed this same faith and moved in the gifting's that are for us from God. When we think of some ancient ones of our time, we think of God's generals: Evan Roberts, Maria Woodworth-Etter Charles Parham, Kathryn Kuhlman, Smith Wigglesworth, and Bob Jones. These people represent many different ways that God reached out to them on different occasions throughout life. It was through their obedience and with faith that they stepped out and were led by the power of the Holy Spirit. Many revivals and movements also occurred throughout time, from the Welsh Revival to the Azusa Street Revival, the Jesus People Movement, the Charismatic Movement, and more. By pursuing biblical stories leading up to today, a shift within you will occur, and your eyes will begin to open. We must keep in mind what the writer of Hebrews tells us.

But solid food belongs to those who are of full age, that is, those who by reason of use have their senses exercised to discern both good and evil. (Hebrews 5:14 NKJV)

The writer is telling us not to allow our spiritual senses to become dull. We must constantly exercise them to grow and become wise in all we do. God has so much for you, and through obedience to His Word, prayer, and promptings, you will begin to walk these paths and receive your gifting's to fulfill your God-given destiny.

Your assignments here on earth will be made to you, and you will operate with these gifts for the glory of God and His kingdom! Your identity is in the Father. You have a place at His table because you are His heir. You are part of the royal family of God. You are His sons and daughters!

We are all equipped with an eternal switch and when this switch is turned on, it brings about the movement of the Holy Spirit. This connection allows us to maneuver ourselves to be in tune with the Holy Spirit. As our eyes are opened, our new eyesight reveals to us how big our God really is. As big as He is, He is full of love, mercy, grace, and compassion for His sons and daughters. He is a jealous God and wants us to come alongside Him and co-labor for the good of the world. That is part of what being a son or daughter is. The closer we grow to our Father more is given to us. It is on His timing that we will come into our fullness. We must choose each day to want to grow a closer intimacy with Him. We see in Genesis the love of God and His relationship with Adam and Eve. He walked in the garden with them in the cool of the day. Adam and Eve knew God intimately. This is part of God's plan for us too.

God in action is what we see in the story of Elisha and his servant. In this same way, God wants you to see Him. This is how God intended us to live all along. This type of intimacy puts us in a place where we can press in and see the movement of our King. Through His power given to us, we can release the kingdom of God to the world, creating heaven on earth. When Elisha's servant began to see with his spiritual eyes, he was living in two realms at once! Part of living in alignment with the Father is to pray to Him, ask Him for big and unimaginable things, and then watch these things come to pass. This is what Elisha did. His rivers of living water increased through his servant. The servant was restored from fear to faith; he was brought into a place of restoration and positioned for greater things to come. You can pray right now and ask the Father to open your eyes to new things. You can ask Him to reveal your gifting's so that you may move in them for His kingdom.

Ancient Training: Seeing with Spiritual Eyes

Blessed are the pure in heart, For they shall see God.
(Matthew 5:8 NKJV)

Having a pure heart is key to living as sons and daughters. We will need to check our heart daily and ask God to reveal anything in our hearts that would keep us from growing into a deeper intimacy with Him. When we harbor things that are not of God—for example, fear, anger, bitterness, jealousy, hurt, and resentment—we open the door for the enemy to pull us down and away from the Father. Our enemy wants to use accusations against us to hold us back from our destinies. Take a look at these scriptures to understand more on our accuser and our Judge through prayer: Psalm 82:1, Daniel 10:12–14, Luke 18:1–8, Luke 22:31–32, and Hebrews 4:16. As you read through the Word of God, you will see many more scriptures relating to this subject, and we will talk further about this in another chapter. The enemy wants to try to change our time and purpose. By knowing this, you can use what was given to you in the Bible to go to court and petition your case to God, our Judge. God never intended us to live in all these negative ways of the world. We were not made to suffer, but we were made out of the redemption of Jesus, and the Father made us righteous to live and carry out our life callings. So when we go into prayer, it is important to ask God to check our hearts and reveal anything to us that would hinder our growth. Sometimes we already know what we may have said or done, and at other times we may need a nudge from the Holy Spirit and a heavenly revelation from God. This is why David said in the Psalms,

Search me, God, and know my heart; test me and know
my anxious thoughts. See if there is any offensive way in me, and
lead me in the way everlasting. (Psalm 139:23–24 NKJV)

When we can repent and ask for forgiveness, we can then receive our gifts. God wants to give you visions, and He wants to take you on a journey where you have not yet gone. How exciting this is!

Spiritual senses give us a deeper depth of vision that surpasses natural vision to see what is happening in the spiritual realm. Paul prays in Ephesians 1:18 that the eyes of the Christian's heart be opened. He is praying for the spiritual to be revealed so the Christian can see the purposes and will of God. As believers, we do not need to hope for spiritual senses; we already have them. We need to learn to put our spiritual senses to use. We need to practice to keep them from being rusty, hence missing out on the intentions of God. In Daniel 5:12, God gave Daniel favor of understanding dreams through visions, solving mysteries, and perplexities. The Holy Spirit within us helps us see and understand things in the spirit realm. First Corinthians 2:10–13 tells us that the Holy Spirit works in every believer's life to reveal the will of God. Our commission in life is to reveal who God is through the Son, Jesus Christ, by sharing the good news. The Holy Spirit helps us use what we have in the spiritual realm to walk it out in the natural realm by exhibiting God working in our lives. The Holy Spirit exists in both the spirit and natural realm. We as believers have the Holy Spirit within us, giving us direct access to God and allowing us to live in both realms at once! We were created for the purposes of God to do His works in the world, but we are not of this world. We exist in both realms. We are beacons, light exposed for all to see and grasp onto for God's will for all humanity. We need to use our spiritual senses to help guide us, making God's thoughts our thoughts. The Word of God is revealed to us in many different ways. He may reveal patterns to us in the natural or in our thoughts, visions, or pictures. We may get urges or stirrings within, or maybe even feelings of different burdens that are unshakable. All of these messages from God are seen and felt for us to take action and move according to His will, for His kingdom. These downloads that come from God enter into our thoughts and being, filling our spirits with His impartation, power and knowledge to help establish the plans that He has already destined for us. To receive from the Spirit, we need to be spiritually minded (1 Corinthians 2). One of the ways that we can recognize how God speaks to us is how He speaks to us through our thoughts spiritually.

When you receive what God has for you, such as visions, you will enter the spiritual realm, and things will begin to unlock and open for you as needed. God does not reveal everything He has for you at once. He reveals it to you throughout your life—a life of sanctification. These new visions will be new ways of seeing and understanding. This is living in two realms at once. You may live here in this world, but you are not of this world. God is our spiritual Father, and you are spiritual sons and daughters. This new perspective that has arrived causes a shift in the atmosphere, and the party has begun!

One thing we must remember as we begin to move and receive visions, among other gifts that God has given us, is that the enemy is now threatened. He will continue to try to pull and remove you from fulfilling your calling that is written in your books in heaven. He wants you to believe his lies, and this is where your vision, prayer, and discernment will help you. When you know your identity in God, nothing will shake you. Even in your worst times, your faith will get you through. This is why it is critical to follow the ancient paths of those who went before us in order to receive from the Lord and also to be prepared for how the enemy will attempt to attack you. Everything we need is in the Bible, our life manual. Those who have gone before us following the Ancient of Days, who is our Father, also have tools for us to use. Our job is to receive what the Lord gives us through the Holy Spirit and be guided to the places through visions where we can pick up these tools to be used for the kingdom. God places many people, places, and things in our lives to help move us forward. Our gifting of vision is a great tool to seeing and understanding the roles of what is placed in front of us for our journey.

Father, I come to You today to ask You to open the eyes of the reader to see and discern what is in front of them. I ask You, Father, to give them visions as You gave Elisha's servant and to reveal the

*gifting's that You have for them through their obedience to You
so they may begin to walk in Your ways. Father, I also ask You
to show us any areas of our lives that they we may need to repent
for, and I ask You to forgive us and make us new. I ask You to
close our books so that the enemy has no legal access to us and that
we may be able to move in Your intended way of our destinies. I
come to You and plead the blood of Jesus over the reader, and I
thank You for Your goodness. We love You. Come, Holy Spirit*

Another example of seeing with our spiritual eyes is found in
the book of Revelation.

*I was in the Spirit on the Lord's Day, and I heard behind me
a loud voice, as of a trumpet, saying, "I am the Alpha and the Omega
the First and the Last," and, "What you see, write in a book and send
it to the seven churches which are in Asia: to Ephesus, to Smyrna, to
Pergamos, to Thyatira, to Sardis, to Philadelphia, and to Laodicea."
(Revelation 1:10–11 NKJV)*

John the Seer wrote the book of Revelation. A seer hears primarily
from the Lord through sight, visions, pictures, and sometimes even
words. These visions can occur in waking moments or while sleeping.
As a Spirit-filled believer, this gift is also available to you! You can
learn to develop this gift and begin to move in the prophetic. Keep in
mind that moving in the prophetic is different from the God-given
call of the office of the prophet seen in Ephesians 4:11.

John heard primarily from the Lord through sight. Seers are
visual, and when they hear from the Lord, they get downloads
that are messages from Him. They often come to them as pictures,
symbols or words that we call visions. After they get them, they are
able to release what God has shown them to others. Sometimes we
get these types of visions that come through our dreams at night.
These downloads can be received while awake or asleep. This gifting
can be developed in us because we all have the ability to prophecy

to lift up and encourage others. You can read more about this in 1 Corinthians 12:1–11.

John's radio frequency was tuned in to the Holy Spirit. God came to John and gave him the unction to see, and then God instructed to him to write about all that he was shown. Because John was pure in heart, he could see what God placed in front of Him. His eyes of understanding were lifted to new heights. God gave John two visions, and they expanded to twenty-two chapters in the book of Revelation. Everything that was shown to John came forth from these two visions. Out of obedience, John answered the calling of God, and his faith increased and rose to new heights. Anytime we see a move of God, our faith also increases.

When we follow the ancient paths, we too will receive what God has for us and what He has for us to be released to others. We are not meant to keep everything that God gives us. We are to be vessels for the world, carrying the words of the Lord and telling all the good news of Jesus Christ, our Savior of the world. In fear, John could have taken a backseat. However, he saw the power of God in motion. Through his visions and faith, he stepped out accordingly to fulfill the ways of the Lord. He believed, and through his belief, he received much more. John's story is also for you today. By following the ancient paths of those who went before us and through reading the Bible, our perspective changes and our faith blossoms! This is the beginning of receiving our inheritance from our Father. Throughout the Bible, there are so many categories of visions that the ancients had. From scripture we see that we can have open visions, closed visions, trances, and heavenly visitations. We can even hear audible messages from heaven! If you are curious, you can check out the book *The Seer* by James Goll.

The reality that we now see looks much different from before. We now have a new sense of being. As we begin to walk on these paths, encountering all the things that God wants to show and give us, we begin to leave our footsteps for those who will come after us. Our imprints is the beginning of us continuing the works of Jesus Christ while He is now doing greater things in the heavenlies. We have been predestined by God to live kingdom minded. He has all the tools for us. He will give them to us as we mature in Him. We are inheritors of the great I Am. Every one of us has calling on our lives, and the closer we get to God, the more our identity is revealed. Through this revealing, we receive more accordingly. How exciting is it to know that the Father has so many gifts for us and that He entrusts us with what He gives us. His hand is on us, and He loves us so much. God is the great Architect, and He wants to show us His great designs because we are a part of His arrangement. We are part of His unique pattern set before us. We must follow the ancient paths and stay on the narrow way to receive the fullness of His glory. Part of the power that God has given us is vision, eyes to see in the spirit realm. God has given us this because we are made in His image, and through His likeness we are to continue the unfinished work of His Son, Jesus Christ, here on earth. John 14:12 (NKJV) says it best: "Truly, truly, I say to you, whoever believes in me will also do the works that I do; and greater works than these will he do, because I am going to the Father."

When we follow the ancient path of Jesus Christ, we begin to look like Him, in His image. The earthly ministry of Jesus was moved by the Holy Spirit. John 5:19 (NKJV) states, "Then Jesus answered and said to them, 'Most assuredly, I say to You, the Son can do nothing of Himself, but what He sees the Father do; For whatever He does, the Son also does in like manner.'"

Our prayer life gives us direction and direct encounters with the Father. Jesus spent the majority of His ministry in prayer. He was in tune and aligned with the Lord. Our lives should reflect the image of what Jesus said and did. In prayer we have the opportunity to learn the next steps. Renewing occurs, and through this refreshment we get filled up to know our next move. I often reflect on the life and time of Jesus, thinking about the time He spent alone to recharge and engage in conversation with the Father, and I believe this is when He received His visions. Through prayer we too can receive our visions from God. When God is our focus, revelation comes into being, and we begin to advance the kingdom of God.

As you begin to receive and release visions from God, keep in mind that anything we do is for the purpose of edifying, exhorting, and encouraging one another. First Thessalonians 5:11 (NKJV) tells us, "Therefore comfort each other and edify one another, just as you also are doing."

Anything that we release after we have seen should never tear a person down. Everything that is given to us is for the glory of God. We should reflect the heart of God in all areas of our lives. Jesus came to redeem us and make us righteous. Therefore we too have been given the gift of vision and many more gifts to speak into the lives of others. It is our commission to help gather the harvest. For many are called, but few are chosen (Matthew 22:14). The calling is put into our hearts, and it is up to us to answer it. The Great Shepherd leaves none of His sheep behind. We are called to follow the ancient paths and use the goodness of God to restore the kingdom of heaven on earth.

Father, I come to You today and pray for the readers of this book. May they have the wisdom to see and be used as You see fit for Your kingdom. I ask that You release unto each person reading this book their gifts that You have waiting for them. I ask that this book be used as an impartation to the reader. Father, I ask that Your living water refreshes them and that they begin to sense a stirring in their hearts, a newfound love for You to chase after You. Father, I ask You to show them who they are as sons and daughters, and I ask that You equip them for the day that You have given them. I pray for inspirations to rise and come forth and that each person You put on their path may receive the tools that they You have for them. I ask for wisdom and discernment to know what they need to take and what they need to leave behind. I ask that You, O Father, fill their tool belts up with the necessary tools to fulfill your mission. I plead the blood of Your Son, Jesus, over the reader, and I thank You, my mighty King, for all You have done, all that You do today, and all that You will do. You reign forever and ever. Come, Holy Spirit

Chapter 6

Ancient Ways: Hearing from God

But because of his great love for us, God, who is rich in mercy, made
us alive with Christ even when we were dead in transgressions—it
is by grace you have been saved. And God raised us up with Christ
and seated us with him in the heavenly realms in Christ Jesus.
—Ephesians 2:4–6 (NIV)

When we follow the ancient paths of the ones who went before
us, we begin to see the connections more profoundly of how God
communicated to His people. As we read the ancient scriptures of
long ago, we realize that we are similar to the old ones who also spent
their lives becoming more dependent on the Father while drawing
close in many different ways. We know that the Holy Spirit came
upon many different people throughout the Old Testament and
that when the New Testament believers give their lives to Jesus,
the Holy Spirit reigns in them forever. With the Holy Spirit living
in us, we recognize that we are living here on earth but belong to
the kingdom of God as His children. Our citizenship is in heaven
with our Father! With this being said, we can operate from both the
natural and spiritual realm at once, becoming God through us. This
pleases the Lord because we share our lives with Him. Both realms

interact with each other. God operates out of the spiritual realm, and when we accept Jesus Christ as our savior, He opens the door to His Spirit for us, creating us to intertwine and work with each realm. We can see how both the natural and spiritual realms work together by looking at the trinity. The Old Testament was designed with laws, giving people the ability to follow direction. These rules were set in place to live accordingly to God's principles of how to live our lives. Jesus became the perfect sacrifice in a world that could not follow God's guidelines. The world repeatedly failed. When Jesus gave His life for us to have an everlasting life with the Father, the Holy Spirit was sent to help us. The Holy Spirit works with us by aligning us up with Jesus as our model. By living as children of God, we can receive from the spiritual kingdom of God and release the will of God into the natural world.

As you walk along these ancient paths, pay attention to the patterns of how God is speaking to you. These patterns will help you to hear from God by receiving His intentions and ways. Then you will know what shall be kept and released to the world. Psalm 115:16 (NKJV) tells us, "The heaven, even the heavens, are the Lord's; But the earth He has given to the children of men."

This psalm affirms the authority that God has given to us. His true intentions were for us to co-labor with Him while having responsibility to rule and reign on earth with pure hearts. The key is to be able to live in this world while becoming more intimate with Him daily. When we take our authority as His children, we have access directly to Him to repent and be forgiven when our hearts get contaminated from the ways of the world. Because we are aligned with God through the Holy Spirit, we know our commitment in returning to the Father for restoration to continue His work on earth. Our humanness makes us imperfect. By the gift of sanctification, through Jesus Christ, we are able to hear from God. As we move along these ancient paths, our minds become quiet, and we begin to hear God's voice. As we begin listening to God's voice, we start to hear the purpose and direction He has for our lives. Through listening and hearing God's voice, we realize we are not alone and that God is with us every step of the way. As we grow and develop while en route, our path intersects, putting us on the same ancient path that Christ once walked. At this junction, our human ears are converted to spiritual hearing from the Lord, making Him more visible to us.

The natural realm is earth. God has created us and given us everything that we need to sustain life on earth. He has given us many of the same things here that He has given us in the spiritual realm to operate with. In previous chapters, we talked about how we not only have our five earthly senses to help guide us on earth, but we also have spiritual senses that give us the awareness of knowing. This type of knowledge is what the earthly mind cannot logically understand. We call this type of understanding faith. Faith can be viewed as our sixth sense. Faith is how we please God and have a relationship with Him. Faith operates in both the natural and spiritual realm (Hebrews 10:38). Faith is when you believe without seeing the things hoped for (Hebrews 11:1). Through faith we react and begin to move. Faith gives us assurance that the voice we are hearing is God's voice (Romans 10:17). We sense or perceive through the intuition of God within us, the Holy Spirit. Both sets of senses in each realm are helpful tools for us in life. When we look back through scripture, we can see how both sets of senses have helped numerous believers in the past. We have a spiritual side to us, and within this intrinsic piece we can function in the heavenlies, drawing closer to God. This is where we learn to operate on a different level. God created us to partner with Him. Through our working relationship with Him, we learn to know what He has given us to sustain life through His Spirit.

Just as the Lord has given us many ways to learn more about Him and how to be led by Him, He has given us many things in the natural realm. We are required to learn to use what God has given us in both the spiritual and natural realms throughout life. When we operate out of one or the other and not both, we become unbalanced and cannot fulfill God's purposes for our lives. For instance, we cannot simply function totally right brained or left brained. We need what each part has to offer throughout the many different seasons in life. We have been created by God to use all our vantage points, and we cannot get stuck into one way of thinking, acting, or working. We need creativity along with logic to discern and make decisions. If we operate out of one side for long periods of time, we may miss the will of God. When we are not using both sides of our brains interactively, we will have side effects leading to burnout due to an imbalance. This is where we tend to fall out of alignment with the Lord. Only after we get stuck do we see that we need God and that we need to be able to move in an out of each realm to properly function. The Lord gave us a brain, an organ with two sides that have different functions. The brain helps make up our physical self. We may be more of one side of the brain than the other, but we still have equal access to both sides to help us remain balanced. The mind is the invisible part of our being. It processes our thoughts. We need both parts of this makeup to operate properly. This is the greatness of the Father. He created us and knitted us uniquely together to be able to live in this world while having direct access to Him at all times. God created us to be in union with Him and with the world at the same time in order to carry His glory to others. He created us to have a wide range of skill sets and wants us to use all that He has given us. We are called here to function in this world and to also receive from the Holy Spirit, therefore making us able-bodied individuals. Just as we need disciplines in the natural realm, the same goes for the spiritual realm. In life we learn that if we don't make use of what we have been given, it degenerates. Just like a muscle, if it does not get exercise, we lose it. Just as we need to exercise our muscles in developing good muscle memory, we must also learn to exercise how we encounter God spiritually. God calls us to work hard in life, which includes taking care of our bodies while continually exercising our minds. He wants us to take time out to put aside the cares of the world to work on our inner spiritual being.

God has given us the gift of prayer to go directly to Him at all times. Just as Moses spoke face-to-face with the Lord, He too has given us the same opportunity. We can go to Him whenever we want because He loves us and has created us for Him. He is a jealous God. When He shows up to meet us, it may take on various forms. He can speak to us audibly, through others prophetically, through angels, through objects in dreams and via visions or trances. When we come to the Lord in meditation, activating our spiritual sense of perception through prayer, He hears and restores us. Remember, our Father is the living water, and He gives freely to us, to thirst no more. We need to know how to reach Him for restoration to overflow. It is out of the overflow that His glory reaches the earth, and His presence is manifested. It is through us, His sons and daughters, that He is revealed to us. Through this supernatural manifestation, the atmosphere shifts and revival occurs, bringing His children back to Him and restoring heaven on earth. This is an endowment from God to us.

When there is no clear prophetic vision, people quickly wander astray.
But when you follow the revelation of the word,
heaven's bliss fills your soul.
(Proverbs 29:18 TPT)

Many ancients who went before us were shown the Lord's desires through visions. They did not remain in the vision, but as a result, they supernaturally received the vision and then walked it out in the natural. They followed where the vision led them. Their focus did not remain on the vision; instead, it pointed to the will of God. When God wants to communicate with us, He may use visions, dreams, and prophecy as pathways to display His heart motives. He is omnipotent and omniscient meaning, He is everywhere all the time. He is divine, mighty, and all-knowing. We are His vessels through which He works. Part of being sons and daughters, heirs to the throne means we are privileged to receive with Him by understanding the power and authority He has given us to reign here. When we know our place with the Father through hearing from Him, we begin to walk out our destinies in our books that are in heaven.

God has been reaching out to His people through various visions throughout time. We see this from Abram in Genesis 15:1 to John in Revelation 4:2, and also to us today. These visions are received as downloads. This occurs when God drops something into your head while you are asleep through dreams, or when you are awake and have visions and trancelike states. You may have experienced some of these times when God has been trying to get your attention. In your dreams, God may come to you revealing signs and symbols. You may hear your voice or wake up remembering certain aspects of your dream in which objects or words have been displayed. You may even remember God speaking directly to you. His angels may also come to you. During your waking hours, you may experience seeing open visions right in front of you of what is being revealed. During prayer and fasting, there may be times you will experience a 2 Kings 5:26 moment, where you see from within, knowing God is speaking to you. It is like seeing a movie reel forming within your spirit; it is an inner intuition feeling.

Dreams and Visions

For God may speak in one way, or in another,
Yet man does not perceive it. In a dream, in a vision of the night,
When deep sleep falls upon men, While slumbering on their beds,
Then He opens the ears of men, And seals their instruction.
(Job 33:14–16 NKJV)

In our waking moments, we often are so caught up in our daily routines that we fail to recognize the call of the Lord. God is always speaking to us. We need to position ourselves to hear from Him. As we reflect on the ancients and their ways to hear from God, we see

His promises remain true. We have been bought with the blood of Jesus Christ. His blood takes away our sins, making us clean while preparing us to receive the gifts of the Lord. Dreams and visions are just a few of the offerings God has for us. It is through our faith that these gifting's will be opened to us, and we will use them to walk out our life callings. Just because we may not be dreaming or recalling all our dreams, that does not mean these gifting's have ceased. To receive, we must believe. It is not up to us to know how God will speak; it is out of hope and loyalty to Him that we receive when He speaks. God appeared to the ancients in numerous ways. He is the same God as today, yesterday, and tomorrow. As believers, out of obedience to the Lord, we are to be good stewards of the favor God has rewarded us with. Dreams allow for direct communication with the Lord while we are asleep. During this time, our brains shut down, and our other systems lower, allowing us to receive information solely from the spiritual realm. When He cannot connect with us in our waking hours, God places His intentions into our spirits while we are sleeping. The more our affection grows and intertwines with the Father, the more we will see how the scope of our communication with Him expands in our chaotic waking moments and at rest. Let's take a look at how God reached out to the ancients through dreams and visions.

Then the Lord called Samuel, and he said, "Here I am!"
(1 Samuel 3:4 ESV)

While Samuel was sleeping, the Lord got his attention by calling out his name. Samuel thought that it was Eli and went to him to see what he needed. After the Lord called his name three times, Eli realized that God was calling Samuel and told Him what to do. Have you ever heard your name being called when you are sleeping? Have you ever heard it in your waking hours? Maybe you have, but you dismissed it as nothing. Have you ever thought maybe God is trying to get your attention? You don't have to have all the answers, but upon hearing your name, go to the Lord and ask Him what He is trying to reveal to you. It may be a sign for you or a call to attention to wake up, dig into scripture, pray, see things differently, or even move forward with something. Maybe it is to pause and reflect on an event. Whatever it may be, go to the Father for clarification. Seek Him first, and through faith, patience, and obedience, His message will become visible to you. All things come in His appointed time.

> *Then he dreamed, and behold, a ladder was set up on*
> *the earth, and its top reached to heaven; and there the*
> *angels of God were ascending and descending on it.*
> *(Genesis 28:12 NKJV)*

Jacob had a prophetic dream where God gave him visions, which involved objects. God was communicating to Jacob in His dreams. God was showing Jacob a connection between heaven and earth and the relationship between the natural and spiritual realms. As in Jacob's dream, we recognize our relationship with God. Also we see the roles that the angels play, ministering to humanity for the Lord. No dream should be dismissed. As children of God, we are gifted with the promise of God's revelations as we come to Him, asking for discernment of our dreams. Jacob's ladder reveals to us God's promise that through him and the sufferings of the Jewish people, the Messiah would come. Later in this chapter, I will reiterate how to discern these dreams so that they do not become forgotten. When we do not rely on these messages and insights that the Father reveals to us, and we continue to rely on ourselves, we are out of alignment with our Father and off the path of the ancient ones. Has God communicated to you through dreams, showing you pictures or objects? What did you do with what God showed you?

> *At Gibeon the Lord appeared to Solomon in a dream by*
> *night; and God said, "Ask! What shall I give you?"*
> *(1 Kings 3:5 NKJV)*

King Solomon had an extraordinary dream. This prophetic dream or vision allowed him to communicate directly to the Lord. He had a supernatural dream. This dream reflects who God is and His promises. Solomon asked for discernment to rule the people the right way. He asked for foresight to understand and make sound decisions. God granted this request to Solomon because he fully yielded to Him. His heart was of pure intent. Solomon heard the audible voice of the Lord and entertained conversation with Him in his dream. Yes! Our God is amazing! He wants us to depend on Him, and He will go to extremes to show us His love. Oh, how He loves us!

Father, we love You so much! Thank You for showering us with Your goodness. Thank You for the many ways that You manifest Your presence. We are delighted to have these ancient paths of those who have gone before us to view Your blueprint for us. The closer we get to You, Father, the more we see You in everything we do. Thank You for going over and beyond to reach us through dreams, visions, prophecy, and more. Thank You for these gifts! For we know You love to fill us full of joy, and we can feel it when we hunger for more of You! You are a good Father. Come, Holy Spirit.

I was in the Spirit on the Lord's Day, and I heard behind me a loud voice, as of a trumpet. (Revelation 1:10 NKJV)

God revealed things to John through a vision, and he recorded the data. The scripture says that John was in the Spirit. He may have left his body in a trancelike state, received a vision, or been in a trance during this encounter. Regardless, God had an invitation for John to see His glory. God was getting John's attention in this state to show him the urgency of what was to come. Everything that we receive and release into the world is to glorify the Lord. Visions are one way to hear from God. Through total surrender to Him, God reveals Himself to us. He always comes through. When God shows us visions, they may come both as images along with His voice. What kind of encounters have you had with the Lord?

> *About the ninth hour of the day he saw clearly in*
> *a vision an angel of God coming in and saying*
> *to him, "Cornelius!"(Acts 10:3 NKJV)*

An angel of the Lord came to Cornelius in a vision, telling Him that God had heard Him. Cornelius was faithful to the Lord. He and his family always prayed to the Lord, worshipping Him and giving generously. He was the first Gentile follower of Christ. Cornelius's story is an example of God hearing our prayers. God sent His ministering angel to Cornelius because of his faithfulness to Him. Do you pray for God to show you more of what He has for you? Have you ever encountered angels? Has God ever given you a vision or dream that someone you know has also had?

God often reveals His ways to us through dreams and different types of visions. Some of these include signs and symbols. When we receive these objects through our dreams from the Lord, we need to pause and see where they are leading us. When we don't develop these gifts God has given us, the door opens for the opposite. By moving away from the voice of God through becoming impatient and trying to figure it all out on our own, we open the way for the enemy to attack and twist our dreams and visions. When we get a kink in our communication from God, it becomes easy to lose contact, leading us away from our destinies. By paying attention and testing all our dreams (1 Thessalonians 5:21), we will be able to reject the dreams of the enemy and hold on to the dreams given to us from the Holy Spirit. The Holy Spirit will give us revelation when we further examine the dream, and then we can filter out what is not of God. We have direct access to God to go directly in prayer and ask Him to explain the details to us. The symbols that we see in dreams do not always reflect the particular object. God often releases to us in the same way we put a puzzle together. Sometimes we know where the pieces belong, and at other times we have to go through a process of elimination by trying to see all the places the pieces may fit. When we pause and reflect through prayer on the whole dream that God has shown us, God will impart to us. We also play a part in this matter by educating ourselves on the object and time, helping us to decipher what God is saying. In most instances, what God shows us will be something we will put on a shelf until the whole puzzle is put together. Only then will we be able to release what God has shown us. Not always is the dream or vision meant for others—it might be for us! As we put the puzzle pieces together, we must thank God for how they click in place. When we learn to exercise these gifts, they will begin to come more naturally to us. Through prayer we can ask God to give us more dream encounters, and before we know it, we will be going from one dream to the next!

One example of how God speaks to us may be when we have reoccurring dreams. Through prayer and education on the dream, we may realize that God is trying to tell us to stop doing the same thing over and over. When we are trying to solve the puzzle, we have to look both inside and outside of ourselves. By going back to the ancient ways, we can see the revelations of God and how they worked through the old ones. We were made to have a kingdom mindset. In doing so, we can use these different gifts that have been given to us to move in both the spiritual and natural realms just as those who have gone before us.

Prophecy

But he who prophesies speaks edification and exhortation and comfort to men. (1 Corinthians 14:3 NKJV)

We have just touched upon some different ways of how we hear from God through dreams, visions, the audible voice of God, and trances. Moving forward, let's take a look at how all these ancient pathways reveal how we receive prophetic information from God and how we can learn to discern these revelations. Through prophecy, the Holy Spirit can share different observations to us such as prophetic warnings, guidance, direction, foretelling, and more. Through looking at the symbolism of what is being shown to us along with prayer, testing of the Word, and obedience, God makes known whether these prophetic insights are for us personally to keep, or to be released. First Corinthians 13:9 tells us that we only know in part. We are not perfect, and therefore we will not always understand the Word correctly. This is where we will need to reach out to others in the church that have knowledge in this area to help us discern and test the Word. Many times this process calls for us to humble ourselves and wait patiently for the Word to take form. These old ways are a part of the pieces of the paradigm created and inspired by our divine Father for us to use to navigate life in His proven ancient way.

Prophecy is an ancient gift given to believers by the Holy Spirit. The Holy Spirit reveals the Word of God to us. God created us to be prophetic people, enabling us to hear from Him. Scripture reveals that God has been speaking to us throughout time. With a deep sensitivity and knowledge to the Holy Spirit, we will be directed to how He wants us to reveal His purpose to others. The more in tune we are to the Holy Spirit through exercising this gift, the more we see the Father's messages written on our hearts. All it takes is for us to have a trainable nature to want to understand, process, and release the information at the appointed time. God wants to teach us to hear from Him. He is speaking to us today, right now! Are we receiving what He has to say? How are we releasing His words to others and holding on to the ones He has for us?

First Corinthians 14:3 tells us that when we hear from God and release, we speak on behalf of what the Holy Spirit has dropped into us to lift up, comfort, build up, and encourage others. A deeper or newfound faith is produced when people are reaffirmed in their current position and offered direction and insight, confirming what is on God's heart. Sometimes we may get a word or a picture of something to give as knowledge or even for healing. The possibilities of what God may give us are endless. Whatever it may be, when we hear these heavenly downloads, we are commissioned to speak humbly into the lives of others, helping God to carry out His work for the world. When we speak to God and ask Him to show us what is on His heart, He responds. When we receive messages, they often reflect the story that the Father is telling us. God is a storyteller, and this is how He often communicates to us. Sometimes He delivers the whole picture at once, but at other times we get just a piece of the puzzle. These messages from the Lord may be for us and also for others. The particular unction that the Holy Spirit presents to us oftentimes inspires us out of mere eagerness to investigate the blueprint of the puzzle. This is why it is important to keep a journal to record all that God has been giving and will continue to give you.

In the next chapter, I will discuss the ancient ways of journaling to help us keep these insights all together while allowing us to see how they unveil. As we receive these epiphanies, many times they will not make sense until we receive more. We do not know when we will receive more; thus making it necessary to record the events so we do not forget. When we make note of these downloads in a journal, we are essentially laying them aside, or as my friend often says, putting them on the shelf until further revelation is revealed. In this way, we can always go back to them, review them, and ask God about them. You may need to ask the Holy Spirit to show you more or to reveal a better understanding of what has been given to you. You have to do your homework and stay on it, or you may lose the opportunity to unveil what the Lord has contracted with you. He is the Great Architect who lays the blueprint designs for our lives. These designs that are part of the puzzle come in the form of lively assignments. We get many of them throughout life just as we get upgrades as we mature more into who He created us to be. Therefore, it is important to be faithful and compliant as builders to carry out His plans.

A couple of years ago, I received a new unopened pack of pens from a couple at my church who said that I had previously let them borrow a pen. They wanted to replace what they borrowed. The funny thing is that I do not recall ever lending a pen to them. The crazy thing is that the new pack that they gave me was the exact type of pen I use. These are not ordinary pens; one would have to know what one was looking for if one wanted this brand. At that point, none of this made any sense to me because I knew that I did not loan out any writing utensils. When I got home, I made an entry in my journal with the date and what had been given to me. I then left it on the shelf until further notice. Some time passed, and on another occasion while attending a class at church, a friend approached me to chat, but as he was finishing up, he automatically began to write a scripture out for me. This had nothing to do with our conversation, but he felt compelled to leave me with this information. He never divulged any clues as to why he did this. At this point, I guess you could say that I was puzzled. Out of obedience to the Lord, I took home the paper with the scribbled Bible scripture on it and proceeded to record this newfound data. I still had no clue that either of these events were connected. I only knew that it would all come together eventually.

About six months later and after many more journal entries, I had a good friend tell me that she just knew that I was going to write a devotional. She did not say a book but specifically said a devotional. All the sudden, all of the puzzle pieces from the past started coming together. I needed not one pen but two for all the writing I had ahead of me. As for the scripture, it was to be the basis of the whole book! You see, these were not dreams or visions that I was receiving. I was receiving words of knowledge. God was using people to put something in front of me to alert me. These God winks happen to us every day. God dispatches continually to us, but at times it can be easy to miss the hints. Many times the Holy Spirit will use different avenues to reach us. Continuing on with the story, these people had no idea what would come forth out of the pens, scripture, and word. Our Father knew exactly what He was doing; His timing is precise in all matters! After my friend shared with me what was on her heart, I put all the pieces of the puzzle together. This was when the activation part of the prophecy switched to the on position. Soon after, I began having dreams of different Bible scriptures throughout the Old Testament. This went on for some time. Looking back, my husband still talks about how I would talk in my sleep when I was talking to God. He would give me the exact verse, and at times I would ask Him if there was even a chapter in the specific book. Upon waking, before doing anything else, I would immediately grab my journal by the bed and start recording my dreams.

Guess what happened? A year later, *Behold! God Is Speaking to Us: A Fifty-Two Week Old Testament Devotional* was birthed! Not only did my friends hear from God, but also they put what they received into action. They released prophecy to me when they did not even know what would spring out of it. We are meant to be the obedient vessels for God, to move about, in, and throughout. In doing so, we are aligned with our King, moving into the place that was originally designed for us.

The story I shared with you is evidence that God is always speaking to us. We simply need to be ready to receive from the Holy Spirit. Yes, it took me time to figure it all out, but God knew it would take time. This book was birthed at the Lord's suitable moment in His window of opportunity. God used my friends to speak a 1 Corinthians 14:3 moment into me. I became lifted up, built up, and encouraged throughout the entire process. Later on, the Holy Spirit told me that this book was not my book but His book for the world. To this day, I have no words for this, only tears of joy that I was able to make my Father proud of me. I could never have done this on my own because it would not have had the same outcome. I did not have any stir in my heart to write; it simply came about through words of knowledge and, later, dreams and visions of Bible verses. As I reflect back on the past events, I now see how I walked in faith and out of obedience; I co-labored with God to bring about His will on earth for this book. First Thessalonians 5:21 tells us to test all things. When we receive prophecy from another, we need to judge all the way through the Word. To do this, we must go to the Father in prayer, asking Him if the Word is from Him while searching the scriptures to confirm the information being received. Sharing with others whom you look to for appropriate guidance, correction, and counsel can help because they can come in one accord and pray with you. We need to filter out anything that is not of Him, or anything that may be added to the original word from God. Then you can ask the Lord how to apply this new knowledge to your life. I am sure that you also have stories similar to this—how God has used you and continues to use you for different purposes. If you are reading this and, for the first time, are being introduced to this spiritual gifting from the Lord, the Holy Spirit is encouraging you with this gifting to begin learning to use it. The first step is in your communion with our Father. Ask Him to reveal what is laying on His heart for you and let Him know you are ready to receive and carry out any assignments.

There are also other others ways to exercise this gift. I have found great knowledge and understanding of this gift through reading *Developing Your Prophetic Gifting* by Graham Cooke. Whether you are looking to brush up on your skills or dig deep, everything you need to know and more is in this book. Another way to learn to use your prophetic gifting is to inquire of schoolings in your area or online. Many prophets, including Graham Cooke, offer schooling on prophecy, and many local churches may give instruction on this spiritual gift. The more you exercise this gift, the more you will grow in the area of prophecy.

Pursue love, and desire spiritual gifts,
but especially that you may prophesy. (1 Corinthians 14:1 NKJV)

This gift that God has given to you is part of your design of who He created you to be. This favor that has been bestowed upon you is a blessing to you and to all who intersect you on your path. God's heart is made known through the Holy Spirit within you. When you act on what has been given to you, the voice of the Lord becomes visibly clear. As you humbly continue to brush up on this gift, you will find that the more you go into prayer and study scripture, you will be able to test what has been given to you with the Word of God. When all has been tested, and depending on what setting you are in and at what time, you can release the word of knowledge. If you are in a church setting at the time, different guidelines may apply. I have found that after reading Graham Cooke's book and being schooled in this area, I now have more knowledge of how prophecy operates in different settings and how to go about it. Remember that prophecy is used to build up the church and people, bringing them into unity with the Lord. Anything other than lifting up, encouraging, or building up is not commendable. First Thessalonians 5:20 tells us not to despise prophesies. When the presence of the Holy Spirit is manifested within us, activation occurs. When we fail to produce what is burning within us due to uncertainty or out of our own will, we risk not hearing from the Lord. We defeat the whole purpose of our being when we take matters into our own hands. We are on assignment from our Father, and through these acts, we co-labor with Him as His helper to accomplish His will.

Angels

> *Are not all angels ministering spirits sent to serve those*
> *who will inherit salvation? (Hebrews 1:14 NIV)*

When we dig into the ancient scriptures that have been inspired and released to us by God, we can see the role that angels played and their workings all throughout the Bible. Part of treading on the ancient paths of those who have gone before us is to acquire knowledge of what is available to us today to help us along our path. God has given us ministering angels to help guide us along the narrow way. God created the seen and the unseen, the spiritual and the natural realms. Angels reside in the unseen. They come in times of need to warn us, rescue us, send us messages, direct us, give us protection, bring judgment, and inform us. Angels can often be seen worshipping and praising God. There have been many sightings of angels throughout history on many different occasions. Angels are messengers from God sent for a purpose. God sent the angel Gabriel to reveal the revelation of Jesus to Mary. Gabriel announced to Mary that she would have a baby and that baby would be the Son of God (Luke 1). An angel of the Lord came to Joseph on three separate occasions (Matthew 1:18–25; Matthew 2:13–23). The first time was to let him know that through a miracle, Mary was with child from God. Sometime later, an angel appeared to tell Joseph to flee to Egypt with Mary and Jesus. Later, the angel emerged to tell him when to return to the land of Israel. In the story of Elijah and his servant in 2 Kings 6:17, Elisha prayed to God that his servant's eyes would be opened, and he was shown an army of angels surrounding the city. There have been many other times that angels have been used by God to fulfill His purposes. One time in particular, in Luke 22:43, Jesus was having a hard time dealing with His imminent crucifixion as the Lamb of God. He was in the garden of Gethsemane when an angel came to give him strength. God sent an angel to Phillip to direct him upon a specific road to meet up with an Ethiopian eunuch, which changed the course of his life. Phillip met him on the road while he was reading Isaiah 53:7–8. He was just in time to help the eunuch understand the meaning of the scripture he was reading and to tell him about Jesus. From that encounter, the eunuch was baptized, being the first known person in Africa to be converted and to witness this experience. After the experience was complete, the Bible states that the Lord caught Phillip away so that the eunuch saw him no more (Acts 8:39). Out of Phillip's obedience, faith, and trust in the Lord and knowing his place in the kingdom, he was used to change another part of the world by moving the gospel outside of the walls of Jerusalem and Judea. In times of judgment, God often sent angels to do the work that humans could not. We see this in 2 Kings 19 when Hezekiah prayed fearlessly for help. Revelation 4: (NKJV) reveals to us that day and night, the angels worship the Lord. Lastly, Psalm 91 tells us that God sends us angels to guard us, protect us, and guide us. Just as we see the different ways that angels appear thought scripture, they may show up today, appearing just like us. We may not even know when we are entertaining angels (Hebrews 13:2). Therefore in the same way that we act in public, we should be in private, loving others the same way that God loves us. There are many more scriptures throughout the Bible that God uses His ministering angels for assignments to help us. Have you ever experienced an angelical moment? Part of our inheritance that we receive, upon accepting Jesus Christ as our Savior, is that we also receive angels to assist us and come to our aid. Angels are not for us to worship; instead, we should see them as help sent from God. The only one we worship, giving praise and thanks to, is our heavenly Father. We are told in Matthew 4:10, among other scriptures, that we are to worship and serve only God.

Father, thank You for opening our ears to hear You and opening our eyes to see all Your wonders! May we be obedient and walk out our assignments for You in this life. Thank You for revealing to us Your ancient ways that are still in effect today for us. May we tread upon the ancient paths and gain more perspective of the plans You have laid out to us. We come to You today to ask for more of You. May You reveal our gifting's to us and strengthen our hearing. May we boldly move for You and bring glory to You in all we do. May You send us others to help us along the way, giving us words of knowledge, uplifting us, and encouraging us in times of need. May You give us dreams and visions of what Your intended purposes are for us, and may we clearly hear and see the narrow way. Thank You for sending

Your ministering angels to us for Your purposes. We are honored that You love us so much that You give us so much. We will be responsible with what You have given us, and we will walk it out as long as we are on this earth. May we grow to know You in a more intimate way as sons and daughters. May our true inheritance be revealed to us fully. May we be upgraded as we mature in You, and may our vessels be kept clean at all times, denying the enemy any access to us through repenting and being forgiven when needed. In our maturity, may we see when the enemy is using others or using us against ourselves to keep us from our inheritance given by You. We plead the blood of Jesus over our lives. Father, we love You so much and want Your glory to be revealed with each breath we take. Come, Holy Spirit; have Your way.

Notes

1. *Spiritual Realities The Spiritual, Mystical and Supernatural* by Harold R. Eberle, Yakima: Worldcast Publishing, 2011
2. *Developing Your Prophetic Gifting* by Graham Cooke, Grand Rapids: Chosen Books a Division of Baker House Book Company, 2003

Chapter 7

Ancient Ways of Journaling

I will stand my watch
And set myself on the rampart,
And watch to see what He will say to me,
And what I will answer when I am corrected.
Then the Lord answered me and said:
"Write the vision And make it plain on tablets,
That he may run who reads it.
For the vision is yet for an appointed time;
But at the end it will speak,
and it will not lie. Though it tarries, wait for it;
Because it will surely come, It will not tarry.
—*Habakkuk 2:1–3 (NKJV)*

In chapter 6, we learned some ancient ways to hear from God and the various avenues of how He communicates to us. Now, let's take a look at what to do with the information that we receive from our Father. When we write down what we receive from the Lord while yielding to this chosen style of communication, His presence becomes manifested, and the story begins to unveil right before our eyes. We play a significant role in receiving and releasing this information. As the chosen ones, we have been assigned to show the world the Ancient of Days and His love for us. He desires us to want an intimacy with Him and to understand and communicate with Him, establishing His ways on earth. Journaling is both a natural and spiritual tool that we have been given to help us process what God is saying. Habakkuk is telling us to think differently about what we would normally do with what God relays to us. When we receive from the Lord through dreams, visions, and more, we need to pause and watch for how they will be revealed. We don't have all the answers immediately because we do not always see or hear what the Lord is saying. Sometimes the story does not make sense because we don't have the entire picture. Because God is a storyteller and often gives us only parts to consider at a time, we need to understand the whole story before we can discern and release it. Journaling helps us to connect the dots.

When we journal through encountering the things of the Lord, we draw closer to Him and begin to hear His voice through our written words. As we record the notes, we begin to grasp what is on God's heart. God wants to deposit His thoughts into us from the spiritual realm and activate them in the natural realm through us. Sometimes these visions will be solely for us, and at other times we will be the vessels to share what is bestowed upon the heart of God. Whomever the visions are for, journaling is the way to bring them to the surface to be displayed. These gifts from the Lord have been given to us to help us carry out His purposes. When we put what we have in our minds to paper and pen through journaling, we can release what God has downloaded to us and receive more of the story. Journaling is the key to having a place to put down these thoughts from God until the time comes to bring them to life. Upon God's chosen time, we will have all of the pieces of the puzzle put together. His story will then be revealed and we will know what part we play. By having the desire to see these revelations come to life, it is through our faith and trust in the Lord that we continue to record what we receive. When our intent is good having a pure heart aligned with the Father, we operate our best. We can receive and release with no line failure in our communication with God. Habakkuk the prophet was obedient to God. God told him to write the vision, and in writing it, he was then told to release it, teaching others what he saw. This ancient one shows us old ways of bringing life to what God gives us. Through faith like Habakkuk's, we will acquire from God and deliver according to His plans.

Habakkuk, a prophet who had His doubts about what God was doing in his time, did not understand how He was allowing all these terrible things to happen to the world. Everywhere he turned, he saw corruption and destruction taking place. He was complaining to God and asking Him why He was not taking action to punish all the unending offenses. Habakkuk believed that God could not see all the horrible things that were happening because His eyes were too pure to see them (Habakkuk 1:13). God communicated to Habakkuk in a vision, showing him that He knew what was happening and that He was right in what He was doing. God transformed Habakkuk's bitterness into faith while fulfilling the vision. In chapter 2, God gave Habakkuk specific steps that would help him to gain trust to be able to see what would transpire. Habakkuk did not see the whole picture. He saw the details of what was happening but needed to receive the vision of God to start to put the pieces together. In the end, his faith was restored in the Lord. Let's trace these ancient steps of Habakkuk to help us understand the purpose of journaling.

I will stand my watch
And set myself on the rampart,
And watch to see what He will say to me,
And what I will answer when I am corrected. (Habakkuk 2:1 NKJV)

The first thing that Habakkuk did was watch. He paused in the moment and listened for the Lord. Just as God was communicating to Habakkuk, He still speaks to us today. Sometimes we get so busy with life that we forget to slow down and reflect on what God is saying to us. It is easy to miss out on the many opportunities God gives us because we are too focused on the details of what the world throws at us. We tend to focus on the tangible in the natural and often forget that God is spiritual and is always working on our behalf in the unseen. We must learn to focus on what God is pointing to. Slowing down helps us to receive in abundance from God. When we do this, we are learning to co-labor with God instead of trying to control everything that occurs each day. Now with having unveiled eyes, we see the world through the Fathers eyes. We are the vessels who carry out His plans. God is always talking to us and speaks in numerous ways. We know that God can speak to us audibly through Jesus, the Holy Spirit, prophets, words of knowledge, angels, dreams, and visions. What we do with these revelations is the key to understanding how we hear the Lord. We must believe that God is speaking to us and that He wants a two-way conversation with us. While we are in the waiting expecting to see a move of God and preparing for the story to take form, we can reposition ourselves by turning our thoughts toward prayer and meditation, anticipating the next step.

> *Then the Lord answered me and said:*
> *"Write the vision*
> *And make it plain on tablets,*
> *That he may run who reads it. (Habakkuk 2:2 NKJV)*

The Lord was quick to answer Habakkuk. He was ready to move and apply the knowledge of God to the situation at hand. When the Lord answers your call, be ready for action. Writing down the vision that God gives you not only helps you to retain this newfound knowledge but also allows you to look over it again and again, seeing the formation of the story taking place. By journaling, our faith deepens, enabling us to see and walk out the calling of the Lord. God is always answering us, but sometimes it takes time to get all the pieces of the picture He is showing us. Whatever the length, journaling allows for time to pass, enabling us to pick up right where we have left off. Writing down the story shows us how it is unfolding and coming to life in the natural realm. Some of the things that are being resurfaced to us from God in the spiritual realm through dreams and visions may need some type of action required. Habakkuk 2:2 tells us to write the vision and to read it over and over so that when the time comes to release it, we will be able to.

> *For the vision is yet for an appointed time;*
> *But at the end it will speak, and it will not lie.*
> *Though it tarries, wait for it;*
> *Because it will surely come,*
> *It will not tarry. (Habakkuk 2:3 NKJV)*

God has an appointed time for all things that He does. When we get any dreams, visions, or words, God is trusting in us as sons and daughters to be obedient and diligent to carry out the assignment on His time. Journaling helps us to identify and understand what God is telling us. When we commit the thoughts of the Lord to the written word, we are essentially awakening them and bringing them to life. God is painting a story for us and writing insights on paper to show us the intentions of the vision. It is not our job to know the purpose of the information, but out of obedience to the Lord, we must take action when God is calling upon us. At the time of unloosing of the material, we will know what we need to carry out the call. We will also recognize whether the information is for us to keep or to loose into the atmosphere. Journaling connects us to God and is a two-way conversation with the Lord. When we write down the thoughts that God entrusts within us, we see His heart. We can also learn to hear His voice when we are interacting consistently with Him. God's design for all of humanity is to be in direct communication with Him. The death of Jesus Christ has made this gift available to us today. Jesus freely released His Spirit in dying for us so that we could obtain the spirit to carry out the works of the Lord. He perfects our faith in the Lord. When we give our lives to Christ, we receive the authority of God to carry out His will on earth (see John 14). When we live in the world for the world, we cannot receive Him because we cannot see Him. When you tread the path of the Ancient of Days, He removes everything of the world and replaces it with everything of Him. Your earthly needs no longer take precedence over you spiritual needs. When God gives us assignments, He also gives us the authority to go. Journaling show us the ways of God. It guides us into His truths, giving us an increasing and everlasting faith—the hunger for more. It releases us to move forward in carrying out the purposes of the Lord.

When we take these ancient steps of journaling and apply them to our lives today, we can be sure that we will see the fruit of the Lord. Walking in the footsteps of the ancients and getting back to the old ways aligns us with the true heart of God. When we begin to tread these age-old ways, we create a change of the sequence of events by shifting the atmosphere and restoring it to the intended design of the Lord. We were meant to work alongside our Father to see breakthroughs while taking in the wonderful future that God has in store for us. It is because of who God is, not of who we are, that we see these wonderful moves. If you haven't tried journaling the Habakkuk way, today is the day to start. Redefine what your relationship with the Lord looks like by trekking along this ancient path. Align yourself with God, seeing yourself the way that God sees you. Let Him fill you with encouragement as He lifts you up, showing you how He loves you! Watch, pause in the moment, pray and meditate, and then ask the Father to reveal more to you. Write what He says and wait for His timing to release it. Watch how God fulfills what He discloses to you.

Father, we want to grow closer to You, and we want to represent who You are to the world. Help us to learn to mature in wisdom and strength as we step among these ancient paths. Lead us into this new experience of journaling with a newfound confidence and expectation of receiving bold and clear from you. We want to encounter You in this new experience. We want to tell the world of who You are. Show us in this time and bring forth a hunger within us to continue to seek You out. Bring Your works to life through us, Father. Thank You for all You do for us and for how You love us graciously. Thank You for sending your Son to die for us to continue in His steps. We will tread upon the ancient ways of those who have gone before us, and we will carry out Your will. Use us, Lord. Guide us. Protect us. Strengthen us. Encourage us. Build us up. Make us pliable like gold in the fire to yield to You and your understanding of what is to be fulfilled. We are Your vessels; make us clean. Purify us in the refining process; mature us into You more each day. Thank You for the gift of journaling, and may we pursue You out of our obedience to see Your will on earth to be done. May You have the glory forever and ever! Come, Holy Spirit.

Chapter 8

Ancient Ways to Live in This World but Not of It

*Jesus said to him, "If you can believe, all things
are possible to him who believes."*

—*Mark 9:23 (NKJV)*

Our total dependence rests upon our relationship with the Father
through faith. As faith increases, our ability begins to work as His
ability. Our spiritual senses are awakened and enlightened in all
the Father's ways. Through faith we become obedient and move
into action. It is plain and simple, we move. We learn to not lean
on our own understanding, and we obtain trust from the Lord.
Faith requires patience, wisdom, and knowledge. God gives us our
faith, and through obedience of His Word, more is revealed to
us. No matter what the circumstance, faith operates in our lives
continually when we see the true nature of God. Righteousness is
obtained through faith. Faith is a choice, and when we choose it,
God gives us tools that come along with it. We learn to expect faith
and persevere through faith, and when we are under attack, it is our

faith that gets us through. It is through faith that we accept Jesus and the works of the Holy Spirit. Faith is the supernatural way of the ancients. God designed it to be this way. Jesus was full of faith, and it was His words in Mark 9:23 that said, "If you can believe, all things are possible to him who believes." Faith will move you from being single-minded to becoming kingdom minded!

To live in this world today, we need to follow the ancient ways outlined in the Bible. Faith is a key pattern in scripture. We can follow the faith imprint that Jesus left behind by reading about His life. Each page within the Bible has been prepared and breathed by God Himself. It is through obedience to the Father, while getting to know Him deeper through being rooted in His firm foundation, that our faith gains an intimate favor with Him. This intimacy is filled with knowledge, wisdom, discernment, spiritual gifts, love and more, given to us from the Holy Spirit. Our spiritual senses become heightened, and we begin to move empowered by the Spirit. We were designed to be in sync with God to fulfill our assignments on earth living from the kingdom for His glory. We must follow the ancient paths of those who went before us to be uniquely grafted into the Vinedresser's vine, while seeing the vision God has for us. The ancients set a pattern for us to follow, and they left us with the greatest gift: the Word of God. We have been given this glorious endowment, His divine word and favor to walk in the ways of the Ancient of Days. He has specifically prepared the way for each one of us. Our job is to know where we stand so that when we reign, we reign from heaven's perspective. Through reading God's Word, praying and receiving from the Father while in alignment with Him, we co-labor with God, moving in victory! Our alignment allows us to live from the Spirit of God, living in this world not of this world, permanently living in two realms at once!

"Meaningless! Meaningless!" says the Teacher.
"Utterly meaningless! Everything is
meaningless." (Ecclesiastes 1:2 NIV)

King Solomon was looking for the purpose of life. He searched apart from God, using his wisdom and knowledge. He was discontent in all things he found and tried. Things only got worse for Solomon. Finally he came to the conclusion that he was an empty vessel without God. Solomon's quest absent from God left him living in and of this world. We are heirs of God, and everything that belongs to the Father belongs to His children. Many of us today move throughout life working hard to buy the latest gadget, the bigger house, the faster car, the best clothing, higher pay—the list goes on. At the end of the day, no matter where we end up on the hierarchy chain of business or life in general, without God, everything is impossible, and we will feel the same discontent within our being just as Solomon did. When we are in accord with God, our searching ends, and we see all the riches that the father has given us right where we are. This is where we live in this world but not of the world. Solomon felt no peace. His focus was on the wrong things. When we consecrate ourselves to the Father, we feel the completeness that He gives to us. He has had it all along for us in the waiting, but our eyes were focused on the wrong things. The enemy has a way of diverging people through materialistic things, making them think that these items will satisfy the soul. These earthly items have no true meaning. The true meaning of life is within the Father, and it is where we belong. There is nothing under the sun that can make us whole. Our Lord, the great King in heaven, makes up our total being and fills us whole with His Spirit. Through the process of maturation and sanctification throughout our lives, we find our true selves. Our true north is when our eyes are set on things from above, not things of the world. When we get on the narrow path of the ancients not veering with all eyes on God, our true destination is revealed. In the unraveling transformation occurs and promotion happens! Heavenly promotions are much more fulfilling than earthly treasures.

Living in this world but not of this world requires faith, which is obtained from our choice to walk the ancient paths, moving from assignment to assignment and trusting God. God loves us and has given us grace and power to live the Christian life. He has also given us access to the throne of grace in our time of need. We can enter in through prayer, repent, and surrender our being while gaining God's favor. His mercies endure forever when we believe we receive the goodness of God. When we walk out of the throne of grace, the light of the Lord will radiate through us for all to see. We carry God's glory, and when we walk as sons and daughters, our light shines among the ancient paths for the world to see. Along our path, we plant the seeds of the Lord with help of the Holy Spirit, moving from one appointment to the next. As others come upon the seeds, God does the rest. The seeds are who we are. Our reflection becomes a seed to release to others. God brings our seeds to life and births them within the believer. This is part of our destiny, the great commission. We carry the good news of Jesus throughout our lives, along with the stories recorded of the ancients who have gone before us. This is our call to action to move. We are filled with the greatness of the Lord, and through His Spirit we move.

Ancient Establishments from Within

Have you ever noticed when you enter certain places that a sign on the door often says, "established"? When we see the writing, we often dismiss it because we know it means how long the business has been in operation. We dismiss it because we tend not to care or want to know about the establishment; we only want something from the establishment. Therefore we have programmed our minds to ignore the sign and walk in to get what we want.

What if God was trying to show you something about this word, but you were too busy overlooking it? It's like when you see something over and over: it begins to form a pattern, which then forms a thought in your mind. How many times would you have to see the word *established* until you start to investigate it? God has established all your ways. His decrees are written on your heart. He did this before you were in the womb. He has your future written out. God has given us free will to choose to investigate what He has put right in front of your eyes. Because He is full of mercy and grace, He tries different ways to tell and show us things. When we are not receiving what God is showing us in our waking moments, He will come to us at night when we are asleep in our dreams. Sleep is a place where all the daily chaos is nonexistent. He wants us to step into what He has for us. He is our breakthrough! He has told us throughout scripture that through Christ, He anoints and strengthens us. God has established us for more ways than you can imagine (Job 22:28; 2 Corinthians 1:21; 1 Thessalonians 3:13; Romans 16:25). Each day, the Lord gives us more glimpses of who He is. It is up to us to open our eyes and take in the view.

The world is a busy place. People are always on a schedule to get things done, but when they wake up the next day, they start with another list, and there is never a sense of accomplishment of seeing any near finality. Often, what is seen is a continuation of the day before. It is like a mouse on a wheel going in circles all day but never getting anywhere. We are driven by daily expectations in our lives, and often we put God on the back burner. His aim is greater than anything we can do on an average, mundane day. When we are looking with just our human senses, we will overlook everything that God puts in front of us and continue to ride the circuit of life. We will miss out just like King Solomon. God, our Creator, has established His purpose for us for this life. We need to use or spiritual senses. Our spiritual senses are outlined throughout the book of Hebrews. Just as our earthly bodies have senses, so do our spirits. Using our spiritual senses moves us from drinking milk to eating the solid food of the Lord. When we partake of the Holy Spirit, we are living in this world but not of this world.

The next time you see an occurrence of a place, thing, or even a word, take a moment to talk with God about it. Ask Him what He is trying to show you. Ask Him to reveal what He wants to release to you. Don't take things that you see each day in the natural for granted but go to the Father and make petitions. Inquire what is right in front of you. By asking God to show you more of what He is exposing to you, the spiritual realm becomes heightened by your request, and more is released. Be ready for God to show up and have a plan. He may answer your request that very moment, that day, or it may come later. It may be something through a dream or vision. Have a journal ready by your bed to write your findings. Then as time goes by, you can reflect back to your pages and see how your story is lining up with what God is showing you. God is good, and everything He gives you comes from above. He may want you to release your findings to encourage, exalt, or lift up another person. Or maybe your discovery is just for you, giving you a new outlook. Whatever it may be, when you begin to have a two-way conversation with the Lord, the natural and spiritual realms collide, allowing you to live from both at the same time.

> *So they rose early in the morning and went out into the*
> *Wilderness of Tekoa; and as they went out, Jehoshaphat*
> *stood and said, "Hear me, O Judah and you inhabitants of*
> *Jerusalem: Believe in the Lord your God, and you shall be*
> *established; believe His prophets, and you shall prosper."*
> *(2 Chronicles 20:20 NKJV)*

Believe and seek out the Lord. Have faith that He will show up. God wants to establish something new in you. You belong to God. He is a jealous, all-consuming God. He loves you so much. To go deeper with Him, it is imperative to recognize and understand the love that God has for you. Everything that you are made of, such as your personality and more, God has intentionally designed within you to co-labor with Him. You are unique in all your ways.

> *For we are His workmanship, created in Christ Jesus for good works,*
> *which God prepared beforehand that we should walk in them.*
> *(Ephesians 2:10 NKJV)*

God handcrafted us for the purpose of fulfilling our destinies that have been written for us in our books in heaven. We have been designed by our Father to use our unique traits to accomplish all that has been predetermined by God for His purposes on earth. You were made for progression, to make leaps and bounds in your life! In our alignment with the Father, we begin to see the many patterns that are forming along the ancient paths, and when we merge, joining to the Father along these age-old ways, we flow in tune to the calling of our future. We begin to walk out what was foretold long ago for us. God has sealed within us gifts, and when we use them along with the Bible and prayer, our effectiveness will greatly increase, establishing breakthrough after breakthrough. Tomorrow is not promised to us; all we have is today. God is attracted to our steadfast faith in Him. When we move in this type of faith, we continually move forward into our life work, never looking back. Embrace this day that He has given you and move ahead in expectation and encouragement from those who have gone ahead, confirming orderliness to the patterns set before you. Open your spiritual eyes to see more of who He is and step into your divine calling that He has prepared for you. Get up close and personal with the Father. He knows what you're thinking before the thought appears. God wants an intimate relationship with you through co-laboring with Him. This relationship allows you to live from the spiritual realm with God on earth. God is spiritual, and so are you! Remember all the ways that God has been faithful throughout time, and watch how your faith will increase as you continually fixate your eyes on Jesus. His footprints are timeline relics that light the path for our destinies!

The Lord will guide you continually, And satisfy your soul in drought, And strengthen your bones; You shall be like a watered garden, And like a spring of water, whose waters do not fail. (Isaiah 58:11 NKJV)

Isaiah tells us we will never thirst. Living waters will continually flow from us. When we take the first step and move out of faith and obedience to the Father, God will reveal the next step. As we boldly move out in faith, knowing that the next footprint will be exposed, we begin to see what is being established right before our eyes! Let's pray to take part in the established promises of God.

Come, Holy Spirit, fill us up. We never want to thirst again. We want to walk out our destinies and fulfill Your vision Lord in the way that You see fit. Please open our eyes and ears of understanding as we boldly step into the ancient ways of those who have gone before us. For we are established in You and all Your ways. Our faith lies in the doors that You unlock, stepping into the unknown through obedience. For we belong to You, our mighty King, our great Protector! Thank You for giving us access to the throne of grace, where we contend to keep our books closed, leaving the enemy no legal access to them and for recovering us to be filled with Your overflowing presence to restore Your kingdom for Your glory. Father, we receive You and the will You have for us. We will boldly walk out all Your orders in obedience and faith. We are on active duty! Thank You for loving us and saving us to do Your mighty works. We love You. Come, Holy Spirit.

May God Bless you!

Bibliography

- Bible.org, https://Bible.org
- Bible Commentary on line
- Bible Dictionary
- Bible Gateway, http://www.Biblegateway.com/
- Biblehub.com, https://Biblehub.com
- Bible Study Tools on line/ John Gill Exposition of Bible
- Elmer L. Towns, *Fasting for Spiritual Breakthrough*, Ontario: Regal Books 1979
- Gary Larson, *The Apostolic Mission of Jesus the Messiah*, Tampa: Xulon, 2016
- Graham Cooke, *Developing Your Prophetic Gifting*, Grand Rapids: Chosen Books a Division of Baker House Book Company, 2003
- Harold R. Eberle, *Spiritual Realities The Spiritual, Mystical and Supernatural*, Yakima: Worldcast Publishing, 2011
- *Modern Life Study (NKJV): God's Word for Our Destiny*, 2014 Thomas Nelson
- Nation 2 Nation Christian University (*Hebrews Chapter 9 New Covenant Worship* The Epistle to the Hebrews Session 1 page 3 section H. The progressive/enlarging revelation of the blood sacrifice
- Robert Henderson, *Operating in the Courts of Heaven*, Robert Henderson Ministries, 2014

Recommended Reading

- *God's Generals* Robert Liardon
- *The Seer* James Goll

About the Author

Michelle Gehrt releases her second book, *Ancient Paths: Navigating the Ways of Old to Bless the Days of New,* as she continues to show her passion for helping others to hear God and follow Him to fulfill their destinies on earth.

Michelle's first book, *Behold! God Is Speaking to Us: A Fifty-Two-Week-Old Testament Devotional* was written to capture the hearts of people while showing the love of the Father.

Michelle is a former outreach and mission's director in Columbus, Ohio, where she served the city and met the needs of the people. She has traveled the world as a short-term missionary and has gained a greater understanding of what people are searching for. She holds a degree in biblical studies and ministry from Nation 2 Nation Christian University, a division of WIN Ministries of Texas. Her motto is Isaiah 6:8, "Here I am, send me." Her burning passion for others to know the Lord and to go deeper has led her into writing two spiritually imparted books for the world.

Michelle is the wife to a wonderful husband, the mother of four adult children, and the grandmother to five grandchildren. Michelle has a heart for others and wants them to experience the Father's love the way she does. She has written this second book to help others to reach and fulfill their God-given destinies.

If you have enjoyed *Ancient Paths*, please take a moment to review it on Amazon.com.

To learn more about Michelle's work, visit her at http://michellegehrt.com

Other books by Michelle Gehrt:
Behold! God Is Speaking To Us; A Fifty-Two Week Old Testament Devotional

Follow Michelle on Social Media
Facebook: Author Michelle Gehrt
Instagram: michelle_gehrt

Authormgehrt@gmail.com

Printed in the United States
by Baker & Taylor Publisher Services